The
Eternal Dreamer

Also by Harold Klemp:

The Book of ECK Parables, Volume 1
The Book of ECK Parables, Volume 2
The Book of ECK Parables, Volume 3
Child in the Wilderness
The Living Word
Soul Travelers of the Far Country
The Temple of ECK
The Wind of Change

The Mahanta Transcripts Series
Journey of Soul, Book 1
How to Find God, Book 2
The Secret Teachings, Book 3
The Golden Heart, Book 4
Cloak of Consciousness, Book 5
Unlocking the Puzzle Box, Book 6

This book has been authored by and published under the supervision of the Living ECK Master, Sri Harold Klemp. It is the Word of ECK.

The Eternal Dreamer

Harold Klemp

Mahanta Transcripts
Book 7

ECKANKAR
Minneapolis, MN

The Eternal Dreamer
Mahanta Transcripts, Book 7

Copyright © 1992 ECKANKAR

The terms ECKANKAR, ECK, EK, MAHANTA, SOUL TRAVEL, and VAIRAGI, among others, are trademarks of ECKANKAR, P.O. Box 27300, Minneapolis, MN 55427 U.S.A.

Printed in U.S.A.
Library of Congress Catalog Card Number: 92-73380

Compiled by Joan Klemp and Anne Pezdirc
Edited by Anthony Moore and Mary Carroll Moore
Cover design by Lois Stanfield
Cover illustration by Višnja Ljubić-Kramer
Text illustrations by Tom Elliott
Text photo (page x) by Joan Klemp
Back cover photo by John Jenkins

Contents

Moments • Master Power • The Right Wave • On the
Verge of Eternity • Show Me Love

vii

Foreword

The Way of the Eternal, *The Shariyat-Ki-Sugmad,* Book One, states: "The knowledge that the true, living Master gives is direct and immediate, coming from actual Soul experiences apart from the physical senses and human consciousness. His words are charged with the ECK currents surging within him. They sink into the inner self of the listener, leaving little doubt about the existence of Soul experiences."

Sri Harold Klemp, the Mahanta, the Living ECK Master travels throughout the world to give out the sacred teachings of ECK. Many of his public talks have been released on audiocassette, but others have never before been available beyond the particular seminar at which he spoke.

As a special service to the students of ECK and truth seekers everywhere, all of Sri Harold's public talks are being transcribed and edited under his direction. Now these transcripts can be study aids for one's greater spiritual understanding.

The Eternal Dreamer, Mahanta Transcripts, Book 7, contains his talks from 1987–88. May they serve to uplift Soul to greater areas of consciousness.

Sri Harold Klemp, the Mahanta, the Living ECK Master helps you awaken to a greater spirituality. As Soul—a divine spark of God—you are the eternal dreamer. You are the creator of your own worlds.

1

"It Matters to This Starfish"

In ECK we recognize the individual as being the whole reason for the ECK teachings. Everything that is written or spoken is for the benefit of the individual Soul.

An Individual Focus

We constantly try to bring into our lives some understanding and realization of the Light and Sound of God. These are the ways the ECK, which is the Holy Spirit, manifests Itself to beings on earth. Experience in the Light and Sound is the heart of the ECK teachings.

The action of the Light and Sound works in our outer lives in ways we often don't recognize. Whenever we are trying to accomplish something in the service of God, we are given help in numerous ways to make our path easier.

Something's Pulling My Arm!

My wife and I went to the chiropractor earlier this week, arriving at his office right before our appointment time. We hoped to be treated quickly so we could get out in time to run some errands before leaving for the seminar. The receptionist greeted us with those famous last words: "The doctor will be with you in a few minutes."

We waited and waited. Just when I thought we would have to leave without our treatments, my wife came up with a plan to move things along. "If I try to save time by filing my nails now instead of later," she said, "that should bring the doctor on the run."

"Wonderful idea," I said. I pretty much humor my wife, even when she has funny notions.

She confidently reached in her purse and took out her nail file. I believe she had only scraped her little fingernail two times when we heard the sound of feet trampling down the stairs and hurrying along the hallway. The door of the waiting room burst open and in walked the doctor. "Good morning," he said, slightly out of breath.

He didn't seem too surprised when we explained what my wife had done to bring him. "That's why I suddenly had the funniest feeling that someone was pulling my arm," he said.

Each of us has various techniques for putting up with resistance once we open ourself as a channel for the ECK. When this happens, Divine Spirit often steps in and causes a set of circumstances to occur. In one way or another, our obstacles start to fall away. Many times—not always—other people go out of their way to help us accomplish what we need to do in order to serve the ECK.

The circumstances usually come about so naturally that we overlook them, not tying them in to the action of the ECK, or Holy Spirit. We feel the ECK has more important things to do than get us out of a doctor's office on time, for instance.

But as we go further in the spiritual works, we start to realize that the Divine Power works even in the smallest areas of our lives. It works everywhere, in all situations, twenty-four hours a day. It's always there to help us—if we will allow that to happen.

Sheetrock Episode

ECKists come from all over the world to attend ECKANKAR seminars. This afternoon several ECK initiates were comparing notes on the adventures and delays they experienced while traveling here by air.

"Driving to a seminar isn't necessarily uneventful, either," one of the initiates remarked. "I drove while my husband relaxed in the passenger seat."

Suddenly, she said, the truck in front of them hit a bump, dislodging a huge panel of Sheetrock. It bounced off the truck and came flying through the air toward their car. It was heading straight for the windshield. There was no time to swerve the car to avoid it.

The ECK initiate remained calm. Very quickly she said to the Inner Master, "Please don't let it hit the windshield."

At the last possible moment, the panel did a flip. It missed the windshield by inches, breaking off only a side mirror. The couple were unharmed.

They knew what would have happened if the Sheetrock had hit them. She would have lost control of the car and probably ended up in a severe accident. But it didn't happen because she had the presence of mind to put her attention on the ECK and ask the Inner Master for protection.

People who are unfamiliar with the ways of ECK might say, "That's just coincidence." But those who have been in ECK for a while know better.

Paying the Piper

There are times, of course, when individuals must pay the piper for karma they have caused someone else. But at some point on the path of ECK, you begin to recognize that you have earned it. You get an incredible feeling of knowing that payment for a debt you have created has come due, and you try to get through it the best way you can.

There are also times when negative thought forms come and try to slow you down or turn you aside from your spiritual course in life. If you remember to ask the Mahanta, the Inner Master, for protection and keep yourself open, without fear, miraculous things often occur to help you.

It Was Just the Break I Needed!

An ECKist was strolling along a sidewalk in New York. Just as she walked past a filling station, a cab pulled out and struck her. She rolled off the hood and landed hard on the pavement, breaking her arm.

The driver jumped out of the cab and ran over to her. A crowd quickly converged on the scene of the accident.

New Yorkers have a peculiar hatred of cab drivers. They regard them in the same light as the horse thieves of another era.

"Sue him! Sue him!" voices from the crowd urged her. "We saw the whole thing. We'll be your witnesses."

The ECKist looked up at the cab driver, but she didn't see a villain. She saw a very worried man, probably a husband and father. There were people at home who loved him, who counted on him for support. She also could tell that he was truly concerned about her condition.

Nervously he tried to talk her into being uninjured. "You know, sometimes people only think they're hurt," he began. "But if they reach inside themselves, they find an enormous amount of energy. You could stand up if you wanted to."

Somebody stepped forward to help her up. She knew her arm was broken, but she didn't want to upset the cab driver further by saying so.

The ECKist could have easily followed the advice of the crowd and benefited financially. All she had to do was take their names as witnesses, go to a lawyer, and sue the cab company. That's often how things are done today—a quick way to riches is to sue somebody. But somewhere along the way, people who think like this have lost something precious.

Left with this choice, the ECKist felt herself suddenly filled with a wonderful feeling of divine love. "I'm OK," she assured the gawkers. "I'm feeling fine."

The crowd dispersed, grumbling. They were disappointed. What right did she have to get off the pavement feeling great? They had a different kind of justice and other goals in mind. Some probably wished they could have been in her position. What an opportunity. After all, since you've already gone through the experience, why not benefit from it?

The cab driver, of course, was very relieved. The ECKist went straight to emergency clinic, where her arm was set and placed in a cast.

Her choice had been to go either for the money or for the blessings of the Holy Spirit that come to one who is willing to go another step for someone else. Filing a claim against the cab driver could have affected his livelihood. To set this situation in motion would cause grief for him and his family for a lot longer than it would take her arm to heal. She was able to recognize the blessing in the experience. "It was just the break I needed," she later joked.

Your Creative Nature

There are times when we have to decide whether to get our reward in spiritual blessings or in material gain. This is not to say that we should turn our backs on wealth. It doesn't mean God loves the poor more than the rich.

Divine Spirit doesn't work that way. We do what we can, using our talents, training, and potential as Soul. We create the best life we can for ourselves and those who are near and dear to us.

In other words, we work within the creative nature of our true Self, in the Godness of what we are. We work as a microcosm of the macrocosm, which is God.

As we learn to exercise our God abilities, we grow in understanding, until one day we too reach the heights of realization. In ECK we call it God-Realization.

Become the Watcher

If it were possible, I would make a list of the points that characterize a God-Realized person. But for people who do not have the eyes to see, it would be like trying to discern words written with invisible ink. Most people could not read or understand them. Those who have the spiritual eyes to see need only look at an initiate who is living his life in ECK to recognize the spiritual greatness.

Spirituality, first of all, is for you. Only in a secondary way is it for the benefit of anyone else. The benefit to others is when they are inspired to try to reach the state that you have reached.

They notice that you are a person who lives according to the direction of ECK, the Holy Spirit. They realize they would like to experience the same kind of divine guidance in their own lives. This prompts them to take steps to find out how you do it.

There is no checklist of the traits of God-Realization that would apply to everyone. This is simply because each of us works within our own individual world.

As you go about your life with your attention on the Mahanta, you are led to think and act in ways which normally would not have occurred to you. This gives you an edge. In circumstances that once would have pushed you into anger, for instance, you can now stand back, take stock of the situation, and ask, "What is the Master trying to teach me through this?"

Whenever something out of the ordinary comes up—a deviation from the humdrum, routine activities that account for most of your life—it is bringing you a spiritual lesson. It is up to you to take the trouble to try to recognize what this lesson could be. One way is just to say to the Inner Master, "I know you are trying to tell me something. Let me see what it is." Then become still; become the watcher.

The White Wolf

An ECKist moved into a higher state of consciousness and found that she was able to look back at her physical body. Her spiritual vision enabled her to see all the organs operating inside the body, with one interesting exception: In place of her heart was a beautiful white wolf. Naturally she wondered what this meant.

Experiences with images can be quite simple to interpret. Just take a step back mentally and reflect on what the image means. In this case, consider that the wolf is a noble, solitary creature. It responds instinctively to the laws of nature and its own personal nature. In much the same way, Soul, at Its best, responds only to the higher laws of ECK. It will obey them without fail, even as the wolf unfailingly obeys the laws of its own nature.

This individual saw the wolf as being white, and for her white represents purity. This means that her goals in life are of the highest spiritual nature. Her whole life is devoted to ECK.

The wolf image is a variation of the hound of heaven. A wolf is more fearsome than an ordinary hound, however. Therefore, the white wolf at her heart center indicates determination. This person is very determined to live the life of ECK, and will do so with purity of heart.

Fountain of ECK

Insights into other people or situations come so naturally to the Higher Initiates. They sometimes just assume they had a hunch. They often accept this trait simply as intuitive insight. But it is actually their ability as Soul to look through the Spiritual Eye.

It is rarely thought of that way, of course. Our science-oriented society teaches us to disregard anything that cannot be explained within the known physical laws.

When I'm writing and can't come up with an appropriate word, I know I can't dwell on it too long. If I don't move past that stumbling block, what the ECK is bringing out will stop flowing.

It's like a fountain that shuts off automatically if you don't keep drinking from it. If the ECK shuts off, it is sometimes difficult to reestablish the relationship with the Holy Spirit that enabled the particular ideas to come through and be put down into words. So if I keep moving forward, I can go back over the manuscript later. I can leisurely utilize the thesaurus to help give form to the ECK inspiration.

Mark Twain once said that *almost* the right word is not close enough. It's like listening to a singer who hits *almost* the right note.

Learning to Speak the Language

This reminds me of when the ECKANKAR staff moved from California to the new ECK Office in Minnesota without the benefit of knowing how to speak the language. After about a year of practice, they've adjusted. They've learned that people don't talk as fast in Minnesota. You can ramble on as slowly as you like, as long as you end your sentence with the word *then*. For example: "Well, you know, it looks like we're going to have a talk tonight, then."

A recently-published book entitled *How to Talk Minnesotan: A Visitor's Guide* could have made the transition much easier for the staff. The author, Howard Mohr, an alumnus of the radio program "A Prairie Home Companion," sets forth three basic phrases that will get a new arrival through the first few weeks.

The first phrase is "You bet." You can use it for almost any occasion. For instance, let's say you're attending an ECK seminar in Minneapolis. You rush to get to the auditorium in time to hear Eighth Initiate Millie Moore, a popular seminar speaker, give her talk. You get to the door with only a minute to spare, figuring you'll be lucky to get a seat in the last row.

You reach in your pocket for your seminar name tag, and it's not there. Then you remember that you left it on the dresser back in your hotel room. You tell an usher what happened, hoping he'll let you in without it.

"I'll try to find a seminar official who can get you another name tag," he says helpfully.

He's so laid-back that you want to scream. But at this point, you simply say, "You bet." You never want to sound too anxious if you're talking Minnesotan.

The next phrase to keep in mind is "That's different."

9

The usher comes back with the seminar official, who says, "We'll have to go back to the registration desk to get you another badge. It should only take five or ten minutes." Inwardly you groan, knowing that Millie's talk will be over by the time you get back. But your best bet is to stand there calmly.

And your patience is rewarded. "You know, I'd like to hear Millie's talk, too," the seminar official says. "Tell you what. You can come in the auditorium and sit with me while the usher gets you a new name tag."

To this you merely shrug your shoulders and say, "That's different." It shows you're not overreacting.

The third term that never fails in Minnesota territory is "Whatever." It's noncritical, and it means you don't have a strong opinion on the matter.

As you walk into the auditorium, the seminar official says, "My seat is way up in front. Do you mind if we sit close to the stage, then?"

This is the perfect time to say, "Whatever."

You should find these three workhorses of the Minnesotan language very helpful if you get a chance to come for a visit.

Listening Closely

As you move along in ECK, you find that no matter what you do, the ECK guides you very precisely. It lets you know what action to take and in what direction to let your thoughts manifest.

In ECK we have free will; we have the right to choose our own thoughts. But like the help menu in a computer program, the guidance we need is there whenever we want to use it. All we have to do is call on it, take advantage of the help that is already there.

Sometimes we become so sure of the power of our mind and the rightness of our plans that we forget to listen. The ECK tries to give warnings to lead us away from trouble, but often we miss them. We are so set on following a certain course of action that we don't want to be moved off the track.

Locked Out

An ECKist who had not yet learned to trust in the guidance of the Mahanta, the Inner Master, had an experience that taught him a very expensive lesson. Hearing of an opportunity to become a distributor for a certain software package, he went to the hotel where a representative of the company was giving a presentation.

He was very impressed with what he heard. When it was over, he said, "This sounds pretty good. I think I can hitch my wagon to this star and develop quite a profitable business."

He went out to the parking lot and reached in his pocket for his keys. They weren't there. He peered through the window of his car. There they were, dangling from the ignition. He was locked out.

He didn't yet realize what the ECK was trying to tell him: This business opportunity you are investigating is a lockout.

Someone from the hotel maintenance staff came with a special tool, and within a few minutes the door was unlocked. Just bad luck, the ECKist thought. It can happen. But it's OK now.

Then he discovered that the key had been left partially in the "on" position. When he tried to start the engine, nothing happened. The battery was dead.

Again, the hotel maintenance crew were very helpful. They jump-started his battery and got the car going. Still not seeing it as a warning, he again sloughed it off with, "These things happen."

He still did not realize that with these delays the Master was trying to tell him, "Don't rush into anything. Take another look at this business deal you are considering. Look at it one more time."

The man felt the opportunity was too good to pass up, and he applied for a loan to finance his distributorship. But he kept running into one delay after another. It never occurred to him that the ECK was giving him a third chance to back off.

About this time he had a dream. He was standing on top of a corporate skyscraper. It was so tall that the height made him dizzy. He had the feeling that he didn't belong up there. He knew he had to find the quickest way back down to the street level, but he couldn't figure out how to do it.

The loan went through, the business failed, and he ended up with a skyscraper-high stack of debts. Only then did he realize that the Mahanta had been trying to warn him against this venture. He had failed to listen because he let his mind get in the way. Now he is trying to work himself out of the hole.

But in the process he recognized something important, which he hopes to have an opportunity to apply when he has regained his financial resources. He will choose more carefully the next time. He is now listening to the Inner Master, which is the Sound and Light of ECK manifested into a single matrix.

Faces of Vanity

Sometimes we recognize the lessons that come to us in our daily life. Sometimes we don't. An initiate wrote that she had recently learned three lessons. They were about vanity, trust, and anger.

She was asked to be a speaker at an ECK regional seminar. Admittedly very shy, she was surprised to hear herself say, "Sure, I'll be happy to give a talk." As soon as she hung up the phone, she said, "Wait a minute. Shy people don't give talks." She was suddenly very scared.

To try to get around the fear, she began to examine the reasons behind it. Reluctantly she acknowledged that she had a very bad case of vanity, which was reflected in her criticism of others. They never quite lived up to her standards. Her shyness was a cover-up for this vanity: She was afraid other people would say the same things about her that she thought and said about them.

Now that she understood this pattern, she was determined to overcome it. She began to prepare for her talk, researching the subject thoroughly and making careful notes.

On the day of the seminar, she mingled with other ECKists and tried to keep her mind off the time when she would have to speak. But when someone said, "The microphones aren't working," she became even more frightened. Her voice wasn't very strong. How would it carry without a microphone?

Just before it was time for her to go onstage, she discovered that her notes were missing. They were nowhere to be found. Though she had prepared well for her talk, she wanted to be able to rely on her notes. Panic set in; her mind went blank.

Then it occurred to her that every time she was in a panic, the window of Soul shut. The ECK was unable to come through with Its message. Without her notes, she had no choice but to trust totally in the ECK.

Nervously she began her talk, very aware of the hundreds of eyes looking at her. What really surprised her was that the audience actually seemed to be enjoying her talk. They were reacting to her as they would to a good speaker. Only she knew what she was going through. Finally the talk was over, and with the greatest relief, she fled from the stage.

She now recognized that the vanity was there, hidden behind her shyness. But she also learned that you cannot hide behind a mask of any kind when you are on the path of ECK. Eventually the ECK is going to take away all your props.

In this case, her notes had provided her with a false sense of self-confidence. When they were gone and there was nothing she could do but rely upon Divine Spirit, she found that the talk went very well.

A Backyard Lesson in Trust

A few days later, she was relaxing in a chair on her back porch. Little yellow butterflies flew gaily around the yard while a mockingbird joyfully sang its beautiful songs. What a gorgeous day, she thought.

As her eyes swept across the peaceful scene, her attention was drawn to the lawn. The grass certainly needed mowing. She hadn't realized how much it had grown.

Suddenly a horrifying thought trickled through: What if there are snakes hiding in the grass?

Frozen with fear, she no longer saw the butterflies or heard the mockingbird's song. Her backyard, which a few minutes earlier had seemed like paradise, was now a place of danger. She sat there motionless, eyes darting around the lawn. She was afraid to even leave her chair.

While she was trying to figure out how to get herself

out of there, the voice of the Inner Master came through very softly: "You trust me to protect you on the inner planes as you travel to parts unknown. How can you be afraid to walk in your own backyard?"

She knew she had been given a lesson in trust. This is not to say she instantly overcame her fear of snakes—she didn't rush out to buy one and let it loose in the yard. But she was able to recognize that the Inner Master had put her attention on the need for trust.

To advance any degree at all in your spiritual life, you must have trust in the ECK, in the Master, and finally in your own ability to survive in the other worlds. Though in a sense your inner life depends upon the Master, essentially it comes down to developing the confidence, through experience, to go anywhere in this world and in the other worlds.

This is the point I am trying to bring you to. When this state is achieved, you have reached God-Realization.

Losing a Watch

The Inner Master had yet another lesson in store for this woman. This one had to do with anger.

Her son went off to the local swim club, wearing the new watch his parents had given him. Later that day he came home without it. He wouldn't admit that he had lost it, but she figured it out. She insisted they get in the car immediately and drive to the swim club in the vain hope of finding the watch. But of course it was gone.

They drove back home in silence. She was very upset at her son's carelessness and wanted to be sure he knew it. As they walked into the house, she angrily slammed the door behind her. Somehow her watch got caught in the door, causing a sudden, sharp pain in her arm as the door banged shut.

She knew right away that this was instant karma, brought on by her own anger. It also made her aware that she was being unfair to her son. She acted on this realization by apologizing to him. At this point, she was able to give him love instead of anger.

In ECK you find that whenever you go into a sharp, negative train of thought or action, the Master comes very quickly. You will not be allowed to kick the wall or slam the door for nothing; you're going to get a lesson out of it. And with the lesson comes the awareness that you have a chance to make things right. If you can act on the opportunity, then you have advanced on the spiritual path.

It Matters to This Starfish

The title of this talk, "It matters to this starfish," was taken from a story someone sent me that appeared in the *National Enquirer*. It goes like this.

An old man was taking a walk along the beach when he noticed a young boy throwing things into the water. As he got closer, he saw the boy carefully pick up a grounded starfish and start to pitch it back into the sea.

"What are you doing?" the old man asked, interrupting the boy in midthrow.

"These starfish are going to die if they don't get back in the water," the boy explained.

The old man glanced up and down the beach. There were thousands of starfish spread across the sand. For every one the boy saved, a thousand or more would die. Why bother? "What does it matter?" he asked curiously.

The boy looked thoughtfully at the starfish in his hand. "It matters to this one," he said.

Sometimes it may seem as though you are but one person in a crowd of thousands. But in ECK, the relationship between you and the Master is always one to one. You, as Soul, must someday get back to the Ocean of Love and Mercy.

Because it matters to you, it matters to the Master. He is always there, doing whatever he can to throw the starfish back into the water.

May the blessings be.

World Wide of ECK, Houston, Texas,
Friday, October 23, 1987

Sometimes animals can help us gain a better insight into ourselves and into truth. After all, truth isn't something "out there" or words written down on paper. We ourselves are the living, walking, expanding truth.

2

Charlie and Moon

All too often we look at the lives and troubles of other people and say, "That person acts like a complete fool. Anybody with a lick of sense would just change this or that and make his life much better."

Another Man's Shoes

To hear us tell it, if we could walk in the other person's shoes for two days, we could change everything in his life to perfection.

We think this about others, and like it or not, others think this about us.

When we observe a person running head-on into a wall, day after day, we assume something must be the matter with him. What he is doing doesn't make any sense. But what we usually don't realize is that this person, who appears to us to be ruining his life, has a purpose in mind. He is on a mission. He is trying to accomplish something that is just as important to him as anything we are trying to accomplish. To him, it makes sense.

The whole purpose of ECK is to guide us as we wend our uncertain way through life, and to help us to figure

out some way to get to the heavenly states of consciousness while we're still in the human body. In other words,
we are trying to reach heaven while we are still on earth.

Heaven, Hell, or Congress?

Abraham Lincoln ran for a seat in Congress in 1846.
His opponent was Reverend Peter Cartwright, a Method-
ist minister who rode the circuit of the American frontier.

One night Lincoln went to hear Reverend Cartwright's
sermon, discreetly taking a seat at the back of the church.
He had no political motive; he just felt in the mood for a
little bit of religion that night.

Reverend Cartwright caught sight of his opponent in
the back pew, but he didn't acknowledge him just yet. As
the sermon progressed, the minister said to his congregation, "Would all those who want to give their heart to God
and go to heaven please stand up?" A bunch of people stood
up, calling out, "Hallelujah!"

"All right now," he continued, "all those who want to
do good and avoid the clutches of hell, please stand up."
Amid further shouts of "Hallelujah!" the rest of the congregation got up.

The minister then turned his attention to Lincoln, the
only one in the room who had remained seated. "Well," he
said, "I asked all those who wished to go to heaven to stand
up. Then I asked all those who did not wish to go to hell
to stand up. Mr. Lincoln is the only one who didn't respond
to either invitation. May I inquire of you, Mr. Lincoln,
where are you going?"

Lincoln rose slowly and said, "Reverend Cartwright,
I came here out of respect this evening to listen to your
sermon. I didn't come here to bring politics to issue. You
asked me directly where I am going. I'll respond with

equal directness: I am going to Congress."

I wonder if he was saying that when a person can't decide if it's worth the trouble to go to heaven or stay out of hell, he can always go to Congress.

As we work our way through life in ECK, we are looking to experience the better things. We try to stay away from the destructive elements that pull us down, make us unhappy, and bring about the conditions we generally associate with a mild form of hell.

Many of the first steps to the higher states of consciousness are taken in the dream state.

The Dream Master

The Dream Master comes to the individual who practices the Spiritual Exercises of ECK. The Dream Master, who is the Inner Master, begins to give the student an understanding of the reasons and motives behind his behavior. Why does he do things a certain way? What accounts for his fears or loves? In other words, what makes this person go?

A Fourth Initiate told me that for many years she was afraid to talk to other people about ECK. She could never understand why she felt such anxiety. It came whenever she tried to share with others her joy, exuberance, and knowledge. Something inside her closed off. It got to the point where she simply could not express what ECK meant to her. For a long time she wondered what was the matter with her.

One night the initiate had a dream. The Dream Master took her back on the Time Track to the Inquisition in Spain. In that lifetime she was a man studying a primitive form of ECKANKAR.

Two people were very curious to know about her philosophy of life. Since they expressed such interest, she

21

began to talk about the teachings of ECK. Over a period of time they encouraged her to tell them more and more, leading her to believe that they were in accord with these spiritual principles.

The next thing she knew, she was being dragged off to the torture chamber deep in a dungeon and chained to the wall. That was how she went out of that life.

The dream helped her to understand that her reluctance to talk about her personal beliefs stemmed from what had happened to her many lifetimes ago.

Journey of Soul

Each person has a whole series of experiences—good and bad—from the past. Our particular combination of experiences is what makes each one of us a unique individual, different from anyone else.

Many of these experiences were caused by our own thoughts and expectations. Right or wrong, the wheels of life were then set in motion to bring us the experiences we needed to manifest our state of consciousness.

Soul enters the human form and begins Its first earthly lives in a state of consciousness bordering on the naive and innocent. The individual believes the best of his fellowman. But as he goes through a progression of lives, he often becomes increasingly narrow and suspicious, sometimes falling under the influence of the dark forces.

In one way or another, he goes through the whole range of experiences. He is pulled left and right, back and forth, over and over throughout many lifetimes. Gradually, he begins to be aware of the pain of living through these experiences of his own making. And when this occurs, he slowly comes to an understanding: He alone is responsible for his actions.

Identifying Your Problems

On the path of ECK, we learn to identify the problems that are plaguing us. The Inner Master begins to open up small scenes from our past. We sometimes perceive these as disjointed dreams. These dream experiences give us a way to start finding out who and what we are.

As we move into the higher states of consciousness, we become more aware of our responsibility—first of all to ourselves, but also to other people. Our responsibility to others is mainly to allow them the same freedom we want for ourselves.

What's the Reason?

A spiritual exercise called the Shariyat technique, which uses *The Shariyat-Ki-Sugmad,* the ECK bible, can help you to understand the spiritual reasons behind a problem you are experiencing. This is true for financial, medical, spiritual, or any other kind of problem. The technique works like this.

First, define the problem. Second, open *The Shariyat,* Book One or Two, at random. Read a paragraph on that page. It will give you one aspect of what you need to know about whatever is bothering you.

The next step is to chant HU and contemplate upon what you have just read in *The Shariyat.* Don't contemplate on your problem or try to establish a bridge between the paragraph and your problem. This is very important. Just contemplate upon the paragraph from *The Shariyat* while chanting HU. The period of contemplation should be no longer than fifteen or twenty minutes.

After you have completed the contemplation, open *The Shariyat,* again at random, and read another paragraph.

This passage will give you the second half of what you need to know in order to resolve your problem.

Over the past few months, many ECKists have reported experiences with this technique. It is uncannily on target.

A Shariyat Story

One woman had been feeling guilty because she hadn't attended a Satsang class or been active in the local ECK Center for a number of years. She wanted to move forward into the higher states of spirituality. She was concerned that this lack of outer participation might be holding her back.

One evening she went into her bedroom for a contemplation. She relaxed on the bed with a comfortable pillow behind her back and turned off the light. Her question was whether or not it would be spiritually beneficial for her to attend an ECK Satsang class at this particular time in her life.

She knew she had to be totally confident in what she was doing, trust the direction of the ECK with her whole heart, and just forget the guilt. This is what she was trying to arrive at.

Picking up *The Shariyat,* she opened it at random and began to read a passage. The first sentence said something about Soul being in the deep, dark recesses of depression. This didn't seem to apply to her at all.

A little further along she read how Soul is always seeking the Light of God. She couldn't relate that to her question either.

If this stuff doesn't apply to me, she thought, it must mean the Shariyat technique doesn't work. And if that's the case, maybe ECKANKAR doesn't work either.

Though discouraged, she closed her eyes and went into contemplation. A few minutes later she decided to read the passage one more time. Maybe she had missed something. She reached over to turn on the light—and at that moment she realized that she had been reading *The Shariyat* in the dark.

The lesson bloomed in her heart, then came through in such an unexpected way that she was caught totally off guard. She saw at once how subtly the Master had brought her to an understanding of the answer given through the Shariyat technique—that she, as Soul, needed the Light. The lesson came quietly, but once she recognized it, she knew it was the answer she needed for that moment.

Financial Blessings

An ECKist who had moved to a foreign country was going through great financial difficulties. Not only had she spent more money than she had planned to, there was the problem of currency exchange. It took time to transfer funds from her American account to the foreign bank. In the interim, she had so many unpaid bills that she didn't know what to do. That's what prompted her to try the Shariyat technique.

First she asked the Inner Master to help her resolve her financial problems. She opened *The Shariyat* and began to read. The paragraph stated something to the effect that there is no limit to what Soul may accomplish in Its unfoldment. Though the words seemed pretty neutral to her, she took the next step and went into contemplation.

Then she opened the book to another page. This paragraph said that unless the vessel of Soul is empty, It cannot know the value of Its experience or the spiritual truth which It seeks.

Since she was on the verge of financial crisis, she interpreted this passage to mean that she had to lose everything. This was not the answer she was looking for at all.

She came out of contemplation to find that the mail had arrived. Seeing the return address of her bank on one of the envelopes, she quickly tore it open. She had arranged for a large sum of money to be transferred to her foreign account. Thinking the deposit would be made by a certain date, she had written several checks against it. Hopefully this was verification that the transaction had been completed.

Instead, it was a letter explaining that the transfer had been delayed by the bank. Worse yet, a large check she had sent out had bounced. She envisioned a whole series of other checks bouncing all over the country. She could see nothing but disaster ahead.

She was so upset that she lost all patience. She had no choice but to go to the bank. Her mission was to exchange five American hundred-dollar bills for the local currency. She hoped this would tide her over for a while.

She never liked dealing with the foreign-exchange division of this bank. One manager in particular seemed to take great pride in making every one of her transactions as complex as possible. If there was an obstacle he could put in her way, he would find it.

She took the five bills to the foreign-exchange window, where the manager took his time gathering several forms for her to fill out. She took a deep breath. This time, she vowed to herself, she would try to work with the best aspects of ECK. She would not lose her patience.

She dutifully completed the forms, then gave them to

the manager along with the American money. "I will be back in a moment," he sniffed.

Ten minutes passed, then twenty, then thirty. She stood there quietly, determined to keep her cool. She was not going to let that guy get to her.

Looking around, she noticed the manager huddled with a group of clerks near the back of the bank. They took turns holding her hundred-dollar bills up to the light and examining them. One of the clerks pointed to a book and held out some papers. The others studied them carefully, then looked at her bills some more.

She couldn't take it any longer. "What seems to be the matter?" she asked.

"Look at this," he said, showing her one of the bills. "On this one, some careless counterfeiter forgot to print 'In God We Trust.'"

As soon as she heard those words, she understood what was happening. She marveled at how smoothly the Inner Master had worked the lesson into such a routine activity as going to the bank, in a way that only she could appreciate.

Since she was unable to get an answer at the time she read *The Shariyat,* the ECK arranged to tie it in with an experience directly related to her problem. Calling her attention to the missing words on the hundred-dollar bill was the Master's way of pointing out to her: You don't trust the ECK. That, she realized, was the root of her problem.

The ECK sometimes works very subtly. Often we do not recognize what It is trying to tell us. We're too busy being afraid or angry to see the humor in the situations that life uses to teach us what we must learn about ourselves.

ECK may not always provide a fast way to learn, but It does provide a sure way to learn.

Pappagena, Come Home!

A woman had a cockatiel named Pappagena. One day the bird was sitting outside the cage, singing, pecking at seeds—just having a good time.

By some fluke, the wind blew the door to the house open, and the woman jumped up to close it before Pappagena could get out. But her abrupt movement startled the bird so badly that he took off, flying right out the door.

The woman ran outside after the bird. She saw him flying higher and higher, eventually disappearing among the trees. "Pappagena!" she called out. "Pappagena, come home!" But the bird didn't come. The woman was afraid she would never see him again.

She ran back in the house and began calling all the usual sources of help—first her mother, then the fire department. No one could figure out how to lure her cockatiel back home.

The distraught woman finally picked up the phone and dialed the ECKANKAR Office in Minneapolis. A staff member, earnestly wanting to help, suggested she try a spiritual exercise.

She quickly hung up the phone, closed her eyes, and tried to visualize Wah Z, the Inner Master. She saw him cooing to the bird, "Come home now, Pappagena. Mommy's waiting for you." She waited throughout the night, but Pappagena didn't come home.

Love and Freedom

Early the next morning she went outside and called to the bird again. This time he answered her with a song, but still he remained hidden in the trees.

Later that day she decided to do the Shariyat technique. Her question was: How can I get Pappagena to come home?

The first passage she read in *The Shariyat-Ki-Sugmad* spoke of freedom; the second talked of love. Together they gave her an understanding of the situation that she had lacked before.

The bird was her pet; she loved him, but she didn't own him. His true nature was Soul, manifesting in this life as a bird. He needed freedom.

Could she love the bird and still allow him freedom? For his own safety, she had to keep him indoors; he was not a bird of prey. Yet, Pappagena had to decide whether or not to accept her love and the freedom her love could give him.

She went outside and called to Pappagena. He sang out his answer from way up in a tree.

"I know you are Soul, I know you are free," she told him. "If you want to stay here with me, I will love you. But it's your choice. You can go now if you want to. It doesn't make any difference to me."

At this point, it really didn't make any difference to her. She went back in the house, totally released from her attachment to Pappagena.

Just as the day was turning to dusk, she heard a scratching on the window. She went out to the yard to look around, and the bird landed right on her head.

They are now living happily together again.

Sid the Horse

A husband and wife bought a horse, which they named Sid. Their plan was to train the horse, and when it reached a certain age, they would resell it. Of course, it never occurred to them to wonder how Sid felt about all this.

About a year later, the husband had an unusual dream in which he found himself entering a crowded bar. Seeing one unoccupied table, he went over and sat down. A man came over and introduced himself. "Hi," he said. "I'm Sid, your horse."

The dreamer thought this was the funniest thing he had ever seen. "My horse in a dream, looking like a man," he said. "This is really wild."

The only thing that bothered him about the dream was that this man had a tooth missing, whereas his horse did not.

The dreamer and his horse got to talking. Sid said, "You know, I love you and your wife. I'd like to stay with you. I've never had owners before who could Soul Travel and meet with me in the dream state so we could talk things over."

This is pretty far out, the dreamer thought.

"Sid," he asked, "I notice you've been limping on one of your hind legs. Is there something wrong?"

"I'm having a problem with that foot," said Sid. "It's just a minor thing, but if you can get a farrier to trim my hoof, I could walk better." And they continued talking.

When the man awoke and told his wife about the dream, they shared a good laugh over it. She thought the part about the missing tooth was really hilarious.

Later that morning as they walked to the stable, they saw a crowd around Sid's stall. The ECKists rushed over, afraid that something dreadful had happened to their horse.

The owners saw a little bit of blood on the door of the stall, but Sid seemed to be all right. The husband put a halter on the horse and led him outside. "If you plan to

30

ride him, just don't put a bit in his mouth," one of the grooms advised him. "Your horse somehow got his mouth caught on the door lock, and his tooth broke off."

Husband and wife looked at each other. "The missing tooth in your dream," she said. Without another word, they leaned over to check the horse's hind foot. Just as Sid had said in the dream, his hoof needed trimming.

The Dream Master sometimes manipulates the dream state so that Soul may communicate with Soul, whatever Its form. Since the man may have totally discounted a dream about a talking horse, the Master changed the image to one the dreamer could accept. This is just one of the ways the Dream Master works.

Understanding Dreams

Not everyone will be able to talk with a pet or with a departed loved one in a dream. Nor is it likely that you will be able to go down the Time Track and find out where a certain treasure-laden Spanish galleon sank in 1524. Too many people measure the worth of their experiences by how much they can gain. They want to know how rich they can become, or how quickly the ECK can help them out of their self-made troubles.

When people have bad dreams, they often write to me and say, "Please stop these nightmares. They're ruining my life." What they should be asking for is the strength and understanding to deal with the situations which show up as nightmares.

The inner state is always trying to tell you something. A nightmare represents some kind of fear that hasn't come to the surface. But once you face the fear, you will find that the energy that fueled the nightmare is used up. There is nothing left to give it power to run on.

31

If you have trouble in your dream state, don't ask that the experience be taken from you. Ask instead to understand what the experience means to you. Ask for the strength to face yourself.

I have had my share of frightening inner experiences. But I have also had wonderful experiences with the Light and Sound of God. We seek these experiences. But sometimes we have to go through the trials before we can appreciate the gifts of truth.

Meeting Your Fears

One morning an ECKist finished taking his shower, wrung out the washcloth, and threw it on the floor. This way, he would remember to bring it to the hamper when he left the bathroom.

One of his two kittens sauntered past the door and saw this wadded-up thing on the bathroom floor. The kittens hadn't seen much of the world yet, so a lot of things frightened them. Sensing an enemy, its fur bristled. It tensed up and got ready to fight this strange animal on the floor.

A few seconds passed, and the thing didn't attack. So the kitten worked up the courage to walk over to the washcloth and sniff it. Satisfied that there was nothing to fear, it finally turned and padded out of the room.

Two days later the ECKist and his wife were preparing to go on a trip. Their bags were in the kitchen by the back door. The second kitten, who had never seen suitcases before, came into the kitchen and noticed these strange intruders standing there. It quickly took off across the room, slipping and sliding all the way to its hiding place under the dishwasher.

The first kitten walked in and saw the strange-looking

bags. Bolstered by its experience of two days before, it went right over and sniffed them. No danger here. Then it raised its head and looked around proudly, as if to say, I've already met fear, and the only thing to fear is fear itself.

It's the same with nightmares. They often may appear as strange-looking monsters. But when we examine them, we find they are nothing more frightening than a wadded-up washcloth on the bathroom floor. Once we gather the courage to check it out and satisfy our curiosity, we lose our fear.

This loss of fear carries over into other areas of our life, too. We develop more confidence; we begin to expand our talents into areas we never considered before. Because the fear is gone, we are willing to take chances and to grow.

And this, after all, is what ECK is about—to grow spiritually, to be more tomorrow than we are today.

Charlie and Moon

Charlie and Moon are members of an ECK household. Charlie is a dog, Moon is a cat. Charlie's waking hours are devoted to one goal: to pursue and catch Moon. Day after day, the dog tries every way he can to get the cat.

Moon is on to him, though. Whenever Charlie comes into the living room, the cat runs down to the basement and hides. He doesn't emerge again until he's sure the dog has gone upstairs to the second floor.

Moon uses a secret entrance, a small hole next to the wall vent that leads down to the basement. Periodically the cat will come up from the basement, stick its head through the hole, and look around for Charlie. If the coast is clear, Moon can come out and enjoy life with the family. On the other hand, if Charlie happens to be watching TV when Moon sticks his head out, the dog immediately jumps up. He races furiously to the wall vent, and the cat ducks back inside, leaving the dog to slam into the wall and fall flat on the floor. Charlie usually spends a few minutes lying there, trying to get his wits back, then he trots back to the couch.

One day two friends, who had expressed reservations about this strange teaching called ECKANKAR, came over to visit the couple. While the ECKists and their guests chatted, Charlie sat with them, one eye on the TV and the other watching for Moon to come out of the wall vent. The visitors had no way of knowing this, of course.

Suddenly the dog jumped up, raced to the wall, slammed his head against the vent, bounced off, and fell down. After a few minutes, he got up and returned to his place in front of the TV.

The visitors exchanged looks but didn't say anything. They couldn't help noticing that the ECK couple hadn't even turned around to look at the dog. Did this ECKANKAR have some kind of a strange effect on people?

The two couples and Charlie sat quietly watching TV. Again, the dog caught a glimpse of Moon. For the second time, the visitors watched him jump up, run to the wall, hit his head, fall flat, and lie there recovering. A few minutes later he came back to join them near the TV. The ECK couple didn't pay any attention to him at all.

The third time it happened, one of the friends finally spoke up. "I don't want to pry, but I have a question to ask you," he said. "Your dog keeps jumping up and running into the wall, and you don't even seem to notice." He hesitated for a moment before going on. Then he asked, "Has this anything to do with ECKANKAR?"

Realizing how their dog's antics must look to the visitors, the ECKists started to laugh. Then they filled them in on the fourth member of their family, Moon the cat, who was trying to come out of hiding. "Every time Moon sticks his head out," they explained, "the dog takes off after him. By the time you look over there to see what's going on, the cat is out of sight again."

The guests seemed to visibly relax. This simple explanation for Charlie's odd behavior made them realize that the ECKists were really quite normal. With the deep, dark mystery gone, they lost their fear of ECKANKAR.

Sometimes animals can help us gain a better insight into ourselves and into truth. After all, truth isn't something "out there" or words written down on paper. We ourselves are the living, walking, expanding truth.

The Sound behind All Sounds

In ECKANKAR we recognize that the Holy Spirit, or the Voice of God—which are other names for the ECK—shows Itself to us only through Its two aspects, Sound and Light.

The Light can be seen during contemplation and sometimes in our waking state. It is often blue, but sometimes yellow, white, or a number of different colors. The Sound may be heard as a high wind, like a tornado or hurricane, or as a flute playing, birds singing, or many other ways.

Every sound we hear is supported by the ECK. Every sound in the physical plane is only the front for the Sound that always is, which is the ECK, the Holy Spirit.

As you sit in contemplation, close your eyes and sing HU, a holy name for God. Sing HU a few times, then become quiet.

Listen to the sounds you hear coming in from the physical world. Try to identify each one as it comes to your attention, and then eliminate it. One by one, take each sound—an airplane flying over, a cricket, the hum of the refrigerator—and imagine yourself putting it in a basket.

As you keep taking away the sounds that you can identify, you will come to the Sound that always is. This Sound, which may come in any number of different ways, is the Word of God.

This spiritual exercise will help you hear the Sound behind all sounds.

World Wide of ECK, Houston, Texas,
Saturday, October 24, 1987

The Shariyat technique offers a tangible way for you to reach out and take the hand of love that is given to you. Use it as often as you need it.

3

The First Year of the Shariyat

In the past people often thought that a true artist or musician had to live a life of poverty. In modern times we realize that's not necessary. We don't have to live on the edge of existence in order to be creative.

More Freedom

An ECKist worked as a full-time musician. One day he decided it was time to reevaluate his goals. He chose to get into computer programming. He figured it would be a good career for a musician. To some, it may sound like an illogical jump, but it was quite logical.

Surprisingly, his job as a computer programmer has given him more freedom as a musician. In the past, he had to sing songs about how "lonely life is now that you left me." Now he can afford to choose the kind of music he plays. He has more fun with his music. He gets weekend work through an agency and usually accepts only wedding assignments. At weddings, the people want to hear only happy songs, and this is what he wants to sing.

Inner Wisdom

The ECK spiritual new year began on October 22. It has been designated the First Year of the Shariyat. *The Shariyat-Ki-Sugmad* is actually the wisdom of ECK compiled in written form. There are many volumes of the Shariyat, some on the physical plane, some on other planes.

In ECK we are generally concerned with gaining the wisdom we need to live this life better than before. We want to live life with more understanding and less fear.

The inner force we call the ECK is the God Force. It tries to direct us into better avenues of living, if we will allow It to.

A New Watch

About a month ago my watch battery started to run down. The light dimmed, and the numbers looked pale gray instead of black. Every time I noticed how low the battery was getting, I felt tired. I was pretty sure there was no correlation between the watch and my own energy level, but buying a new battery couldn't hurt.

The next time I put on my watch and started to tuck the strap into the loop that holds it against my wrist, I realized the loop was missing. So not only was the battery running down, the watch's leather band flapped around. I decided it was time for a new watch.

I wanted a model that had a calculator. This would make currency conversions much easier when I was traveling in other countries. So I visited a number of stores and looked at several different styles. Most were too fancy. I couldn't find a basic watch that did the job, like the one I was replacing.

A week later I went to another store where the prices are very low. By now the watch I had was barely functioning.

I went to the watch counter where two customers were trying on jewelry. First they would carefully examine each piece, turning it this way and that. Then they would talk about it for a while. Finally they would put it down and ask to see something else.

The clerks were absorbed with these two customers; they didn't seem to notice me at all. After a few minutes, I left the counter and strolled around the store to give them time to finish.

Five minutes later I returned to find the customers gone. One of the clerks was behind the counter, unpacking boxes. Seeing me there, she quickly stood up, and I started to tell her what I wanted. Just then the two customers came back, and the clerk immediately turned her attention to them. I was really miffed at being ignored again.

By now the seminar was just a few days away, and I wanted to have a working watch before I left for the trip. The quickest way seemed to be to find a new battery for my old watch. I went to another store, where I was greeted by an eager salesperson. When I told her what I wanted, she lost interest.

"There's a watch shop in the basement of the mall," she said. "I think you'd be better off going down there."

Putting Opinions Aside

In the basement I found a very small watch-repair shop run by one man. The lack of customers made me wonder how he managed to scratch out a living. But he turned out to be very good at what he did.

"She sent you down here because your watch is cheap; it's hard to get a part for it," he said. "I can fix it for you." He disappeared into the back room, put a new battery in

41

my watch, and even fixed the band. All in about five minutes.

Sometimes we have strong opinions about what we need. We're certain that something shiny and new has to be better. But when the man fixed my old watch at a fraction of the cost of a new one, I realized the ECK had led me to the best possible option.

My old watch may be inexpensive, but it holds better time than some of the more costly models. I'm very happy with it. We've been through a lot together.

Transitions

As we enter the Year of the Shariyat, we are coming out of the Year of the Arahata. In ECK there is no sharp breakoff point between the themes of one spiritual year and the next, any more than there is between the inner planes of God. The transition from one to another occurs in a very smooth manner.

The Arahata is the ECK teacher. During the Year of the Arahata, many ECKists learned that being an ECK teacher means more than simply showing up for a Satsang class with a set course of study. They found that one can be a teacher of ECK in or out of class.

Arahatas serve wherever someone needs to learn about ECK. It can happen in such a low-key way that the person doesn't even know what he is being given. He gains the truth and wisdom that will help him resolve a problem and make his life better.

How to Melt Obstacles

This past summer, the ECKists in Paris invited a RESA, a Regional ECK Spiritual Aide, to be the guest speaker at their seminar. The RESA accepted the invitation and made plane reservations to travel to France. But when he and his wife got to the airport for the flight to Paris, they ran into an unexpected snag.

"I can't sell you the ticket," the clerk said. "The French government has a new law that you must have a visa to enter the country."

The ECKist asked the clerk if he could use her phone to call Paris. Reaching the RESA of France, he explained his predicament. "Can you talk with the customs officials to see if anything can be done?" he asked. "If not, I won't be able to get a visa in time for the seminar."

The RESA in Paris asked to speak with the clerk. The clerk was able to tell him who to contact to resolve this problem. The RESA said he would be back in touch after he made a couple of calls.

The clerk said to the ECKist, "I'm afraid you're not going to be able to get to Paris without a visa."

The ECKist and his wife merely smiled. "We're going to walk around the airport and look for some friends. Please let us know if you hear anything," they said.

A little while later the clerk came running up to them, waving a sheet of paper. "This telex just came in," she said. "You've been issued a temporary visa. Present it at the passport-control desk when you arrive in Paris, and they'll let you through." Then she added, "This has never happened before. I don't know how you managed it."

The ECKist and his wife were escorted to the front of a long line of passengers waiting to board the plane. They got to Paris in time for the seminar, and he was able to give his talk.

Everything was not exactly roses for the rest of the trip. But as they ran into new delays, he kept his attention on the Inner Master, the Mahanta. He found that each obstacle melted away as easily as the visa problem had.

Problems were resolved with such ease simply because this individual was willing to serve as a teacher for ECK. First he did what he could on his own. Then Divine Spirit began to arrange the miracle that would get him and his wife to their destination.

Inner Arahata

Many ECK Arahatas also work in the dream state. One initiate often found herself on the inner planes carrying a child down a white corridor. Her charge was a young ECKist she also knew in her outer life. Afflicted with muscular dystrophy since birth, he had almost no control over his muscles. Since he was also totally deaf, his only means of communication was sign language.

On the inner planes the ECKist would carry the boy to a pool and place him in the water. In preparation for his transition to the other side, he was able to get used to swimming and movement unhindered by his physical condition. The ECKist noticed that in each dream the boy got sicker and sicker.

One day at an Afternoon with ECK, she saw the boy in his wheelchair by a window. He was looking out at the ocean. Suddenly he signed to his mother, "I swim. I swim." Though he had never been swimming out here, he was aware of what the Arahata was teaching him on the inner planes and remembered it as a pleasant experience.

As people are about to make the move from this world to the other planes, they often receive inner help to smooth the experience of death, or translation. It can be very easy and natural when there is no fear.

A short time later, the boy became very ill. Before he translated he signed to his mother, "I'm finished." His expression was very peaceful and calm. His doctors remarked that they had never seen a patient with his condition go over so easily.

The ECKist was grateful that she had been allowed to be an Arahata for this young boy in the other worlds. She was able to help him understand that there was a greater meaning to life than his physical limitations. He was shown that life continues on the other side, more beautiful than here. The apparent separation, the veil of death, is only an illusion.

The White Bird

An ECK initiate was very depressed. She was going through a financial strain, plus the responsibility of caring for her ninety-year-old mother had fallen on her shoulders.

The elderly woman lived in another section of town. She was very demanding. She would call her daughter several times a day, wanting this or that done right away. She was always complaining about something, and her daughter was just about at the end of her patience.

In contemplation one day, the daughter asked the Mahanta for help in shaking this depression. Then she drifted off to sleep, only to be jolted awake by the ringing phone. It was her mother.

"I want you to mail a letter for me as quickly as possible," the older woman said. The ECKist started to protest. "It has to go out today!" her mother insisted.

Looking out the window at the cold, rainy day, the ECKist reluctantly agreed to come right over. She didn't yet realize that the ECK was working through her mother to give her a healing from the cares that weighed her down.

She drove to her mother's, got the letter, and headed for the post office. On the way she saw a large white bird standing in the middle of the street. It didn't move out of the way as she approached. She steered the car around it very carefully, not wanting to hurt it.

After she mailed the letter, she came back along the same route. The bird hadn't budged. There must be something wrong with it, she thought. If it stays in the road much longer, it's going to get hit by a car.

She got out of the car, taking a light coat she had with her. Very gently she placed it around the bird. Then she carried it back to the car and set it on the passenger seat. The bird was quiet the whole time. It seemed to be sick. She decided to take it home and nurse it back to health.

A Shift in Attention

Without realizing it, the woman had shifted her attention away from herself. Her constant self-pity had directed all her energies back in upon herself, feeding her depression. Once she became concerned about something other than herself, she was able to forget about her own troubles.

At home, she parked the car and carried the white bird inside. Upstairs she found an old birdcage. She placed the bird inside and gave it some food.

"There's a bird upstairs," she said to her son as he came in the door. "It's so sick it can hardly move."

Her son went upstairs to take a look. A minute later he called down to her, "Mother, I thought you said the bird was sick. It just flew out of the cage."

Running upstairs, she found the bird perched on the curtain rod. "Maybe it isn't sick," she said. "But it's such a cold, wet night that I'm going to keep it here until morning, just to make sure it's OK."

The next morning she took the bird to a wooded lot near her home and let it go. Watching it fly away, she

46

realized that her depression had eased.

Soon after that her mother fell and broke several bones. Many of the nursing chores fell to the ECKist and her sister, and with her regular work schedule, the ECKist barely had a moment to herself.

If her mother had been demanding before, she was impossible now. She expected her daughters to be with her every day. The ECKist tried her best to please her mother, but it got worse and worse.

Surrendering Problems

One night she fell into bed, exhausted from another endless day. Her mother was running her ragged. I cannot take one more step, she thought. This is more than I can stand. "Mahanta," she said, "please take this situation over. I simply cannot go on this way." Then she closed her eyes and promptly fell asleep.

The following day she went to visit her mother. "I had a most restful night," the elderly woman said unexpectedly. "I don't know why, but I'm feeling pretty good."

That day her mother's heavy complaining stopped for good. She still had her little complaints—you don't get out of the habit overnight—but she no longer blew every incident way out of proportion.

The ECK initiate recognized the help she had been given. She remembered the day her mother had wanted the letter mailed and the errand that led her to the white bird. Helping the bird had relieved some of her depression.

When she was finally able to admit that she could no longer carry the load by herself, things really changed. When the ECKist finally released the situation to the Inner Master, her mother had an inner experience that left her in good spirits for the first time in many months.

A short time later the mother was moved to a warm, homey place where she was happy and made new friends. Within a matter of months, the whole situation had turned around.

You, as a channel for Divine Spirit, often touch people. Because of you, changes occur in them which allow their lives to be made better. But it works only to the degree that you can step back and let the inner power work through you. The inner power is love.

Is This Really My Cat?

Many ECKists have used the Shariyat technique to solve problems. It's given in several ECK books. One woman tried this technique after her female cat died. A very strong love bond had formed between them in the eleven years they were together. The woman missed her friend a lot.

The cat had been gone for about a year when the woman had a series of very vivid dreams. In one dream, someone told her, "Your cat is going to reincarnate on Monday, July 31."

How nice, she said to herself when she woke up. But now that I've moved to a city apartment, I don't know how my cat will ever find me.

A few days later she had a second dream. She was shown two kittens, both striped. One was a light color and the other darker. "The darker kitten is yours," the Inner Master told her.

Later that week one of her friends called. "Two of my cats had litters at the same time," she said. "You're welcome to come over and pick one out."

The ECKist told her friend about the dream and said she would be right over. As soon as she saw the dark striped kitten in the first litter, she knew it was hers. But when her friend said, "It's a male," she had second thoughts.

"My cat was a very feminine female," the ECKist said. "I can't see her coming back as a male. I must have misunderstood the dream."

"If you want a female, let's look at the other litter," her friend said. "There's a very affectionate grey-and-white striped kitten that you might like."

The cuddly little kitten was affectionate, but not to the ECKist. "Maybe I'd better stick with the striped kitten in the first litter," the ECKist said. She went over to look at it again. "What's the mother cat's name?" she asked conversationally.

"Z," her friend said.

Z is another name for the Inner Master, Wah Z. "Let me think this over," she said.

Later, during her contemplation, she reached for *The Shariyat-Ki-Sugmad.* "Is this really my cat?" she wanted to know. "Would she come back as a male?"

To do the Shariyat technique, she opened *The Shariyat* at random and began to read. "Soul will alternate between male and female bodies," the passage explained, "each time learning some lessons while gathering karma and working off karma."

The woman had the answer she needed.

ECK Newscast

A Fifth Initiate in ECK wrote to me about a peculiar dream she had recently. In the dream, she and a Sixth Initiate worked at a TV station. The newscaster, who was not an ECKist, was talking informally on the air about ECKANKAR. "ECKANKAR has been in the news a lot of late," he said. "Things are changing so fast that we can barely keep up with it all. So here at this station, we are doing something about it.

"As most of our viewers know," he continued, "we have two ECKists on staff. To make sure we keep on top of the news about ECKANKAR, we are assigning the Fifth Initiate to be our new weather forecaster. The weather is changing all the time too. The other ECKist, a Sixth Initiate, is going to be put to work in the back room packing boxes.

"We had to make sure they weren't both out here in front of the camera," he concluded with a chuckle. "Because wherever these two go, things speed up."

The newscaster's casual, friendly comments suggested that ECKANKAR was a natural part of the people's lives on that plane. This told the dreamer that many people on the inner planes were already familiar with ECKANKAR. Because of the spiritual principle "as above, so below," she knew that someday it would be as well known on earth as it is on the inner planes. It would also be as accepted.

The Sound Room

A woman who was going through a very troubled time in her life sat down one morning to figure out what to do about it. The idea came to her to write an initiate report. When things get too heavy, this invites Divine Spirit to begin working them out.

But as she began to write about her situation, she became so depressed that she couldn't finish the letter. Laying down the pen, she decided to go into contemplation. She closed her eyes and put her attention on the Mahanta.

The next thing she knew, she was walking on one of the inner planes with the Inner Master, Wah Z. They entered a beautiful Temple of Golden Wisdom, and he led her to a room. "This is the Sound room," he explained. "Would you like a Sound healing?"

"Sure," the ECKist said.

He told her to climb up on a large stone table and stretch out on her back. As she lay there, she began to feel the Sound Current of ECK coming through. It felt very soothing, as if all her inner bodies were being massaged. Soon she was calm and relaxed. As the transformation took place, the depression began to leave her.

Then she sensed the Sound Current raising her from the table. She was lifted up to the ceiling and out through a small opening into the higher states where the Sound Current was much more refined. She felt the remainder of her depression gradually leaving her, until it was gone. She came out of the short contemplation feeling completely changed.

The exercise helped her because she had done as much as she could on her own first. The initiate report she had started to write was the trigger that opened her consciousness. She was able to accept the nudge to go into contemplation.

In contemplation, the Mahanta could take her to an inner temple of healing. There the Sound Current, which is the Voice of God, could directly enter her inner bodies and begin to put them into balance. The balance always starts on the inner planes, then works its way out to the physical plane.

Life may be difficult for her tomorrow, but now the woman knows about the Sound room in the Temple of Golden Wisdom. She can ask to go there anytime.

Divine Help

These stories may help you understand why and how the ECK, the Holy Spirit, works in your life. It is always working, whether you know it or not.

Before an individual comes to ECK, he often doesn't recognize the divine help that is around him all the time. It is always trying to show him how to make his life better and how to avoid unnecessary troubles.

In ECK he learns to reach the higher state of consciousness which allows him to accept the help that is being given. And because ECK is love, the help is a gift of love. The inner experiences are important and our daily life is important, but never more so than when we are filled with love.

The Shariyat technique offers a tangible way for you to reach out and take the hand of love that is given to you. Use it as often as you need it.

World Wide of ECK, Houston, Texas,
Sunday, October 25, 1987

"I tell them that the greatest love I can give to others is to grant them the space to be themselves."

4

The Greatest Love

My daughter and I used to enjoy passing the time at video parlors. On one video game, my goal was to make the top score for that machine. Then I would get my initials posted on the board. I play under the pseudonym *ECK,* which means Holy Spirit. When I do something well, I like to show that Spirit and I go hand in hand.

Being a Good Parent

At fourteen, my daughter's getting past the stage where she likes video games. "Next year," she said, "I'll be a woman."

"A woman?" I asked.

"When you're fifteen," she explained, "people see you as more than just a girl." But since she's just fourteen, she's willing to wait another eleven months to be considered a woman.

I try to be a good parent and listen patiently to my daughter. It's not always easy. Sometimes I feel left out. "Let's talk about video games," I'll say. She's tolerant, but she'd much rather talk about boys.

Parents have to remember that they themselves were teenagers. They too went through that confused, muddled state of puppy love. They survived. Children are merely going through the same stages on the way to adulthood.

Recently my daughter announced that she thought fourteen was old enough to start dating. "Last year we used to talk about grades and studies," I reminded her. "Do you realize how seldom we ever talk about that anymore?"

"But, Dad, these days everybody goes on dates in their first year of high school," she informed me. What she meant was, As opposed to when you went, ancient one.

Sometimes the greatest love a parent can show a child is just to listen. Often this can be difficult. As the adult who has been through something, you can see further into the future than your child can. You can see a lot of heartache ahead as your child takes uncertain steps toward trying to find human love. Yet, human love is one of the first steps to divine love.

I try to see the ECK in expression in my daughter as she goes through the learning process. After all, children are young only in the physical body. As Soul, they have been here many times, going through the changes from childhood to adulthood even as you and I have.

What Really Counts

Anyone who plays video games for a while learns that each machine has its quirks. The top score on one machine in one video parlor doesn't count anywhere else.

Life in ECK is that way, too. We don't count on the glories of past lives. It's pointless to say, "I was royalty in Spain two centuries ago. A lot of people bowed down to me." That doesn't count now. What counts is this video game, this parlor, this lifetime.

Eventually I became proficient enough at the video game called "Star Wars" to try to top Ace's score. Ace had an unbelievably high score.

Over a period of time I moved up to third place, then second. It took a year, but finally the day came. I got an incredibly high score, and I beat him. Now, I thought, *ECK* would be displayed for all to see.

Unlike many machines, this one does not list the initials on the electronic scoreboard. The video parlor's policy is to punch out letters and numbers on a strip of tape. The tape with the new high score is placed on the machine.

After that game, I went straight to the manager's office. "I just beat Ace on Star Wars," I announced, all humility aside. "Could you put my score on the machine?"

"What's your name?" an attendant asked.

"It's not a name, exactly. Just put *ECK.*"

I didn't return to the video parlor until three days later. The tape with *ECK* was posted, but the numbers were punched on top of each other. You couldn't read the score.

Seeking out the attendant, I asked if he could print out the score correctly. I even wrote it out for him. The man was very obliging, and soon a clearer printout was posted.

It took me practically a year to reach the high score on that machine. It also took a few tries to get it recorded in the name of ECK.

At times the Star Wars video game works almost like an oracle for me. Sometimes I tell my wife, "I'm going down to the oracle." Usually I have a pretty good idea of how things are going and how to work with them. But if I put my full attention on the game, it occupies the mind, and through the game the ECK shows me what to do.

Video games can teach you a lot. Just like life, they have level after level of progress.

Spiritual Plateaus

Sometimes an ECKist will write, "I feel I have come to an end. I'm a Third [or Fourth, or whatever] Initiate. It seems I'm making no spiritual progress at all. I would like more experiences with the Light and Sound of God, like I used to have in the Second Initiation. Why isn't it happening now? What's the matter?"

This person has come to a plateau. Life has all kinds of plateaus. You can climb up the mountain for just so long, and then you come to an area of level ground. This is necessary—you can't keep going uphill all the time.

A person must then make his way across the plateau to the next set of stairs. Often he is impatient. Before he has a right to expect to continue upward, he's saying, "This is dull. Where are the next steps?"

By keeping him on level ground for a while, the Master is merely trying to tell him, "Be patient. When you have taken enough steps across that plateau, you will find the flight of stairs that will take you up to the next level of spiritual realization."

Impatience makes people frantic. They start talking and complaining so much that they shut off the inner hearing. When the mouth is working, the ears can't hear.

How to Play the Game

There is a particular way to get through each level of progress in life, as in video games. First you have to identify the obstacles. Then you figure out how to overcome them. The only way to jump ahead is to learn how to turn the corners, evade and sidestep the obstacles, and so on. You keep doing these things until all the factors are right, until you understand the game.

When all the factors are right, you can get through the obstacles and reach the end of that game, that plateau. Only at this point does the game shift, signaling that you are now ready to start a whole new game.

A new player often finds himself surrounded by minimasters—old hands at the game who are all too ready to tell him exactly what to do. "Watch out!" they'll yell. "Jump. Don't jump. Turn left there. Go through that tunnel. If you go to the right, you won't make it." They'll try to tell you what to do every step of the way.

But when you reach a certain level of spiritual unfoldment, you are actually near the forefront of those who are walking the spiritual path. The only one walking with you now is the Inner Master, whose voice is very subtle. You have to learn to listen carefully for the instructions—when to go left, go right, halt, or advance double-time.

The instructions given by the Inner Master are perceived as nudges, feelings, or intuition. Sometimes they come as direct experiences through the dream state, Soul Travel, or any number of different ways. When you listen to them, you know directly what steps to take in order to get through that level of unfoldment.

The farther you go, the fewer maps are available to chart the path. There are fewer travelers. There are fewer players to tell you what to look for, what to watch out for. It is up to you to keep your eyes wide open and stay alert to the guidance of the ECK.

You can no longer rely on memory and established patterns. The rules change so quickly that you can only go by your inner direction.

This is the way of life for the individual on the path home to God. This is also what makes the path of ECK different from many other religions.

Many Different Heavens

Other religious paths are usually based on divine scripture. As long as the followers read and live by the moral tenets contained in their particular scriptures, they are told they will go to heaven when they leave this life.

Rarely are they told by the leaders that there's no guarantee which heaven they will reach. No one mentions that there is more than just one heaven. There are many different levels. The heaven they get to may not be the highest one. Saint Paul spoke of being caught up into the third heaven, but there are heavens upon heavens beyond that.

Better Spiritual Mileage

Before coming to ECK, most people are at the first, second, or third level of the video game of life. They are just starting. They are learning a lot and having a good time.

Beginners at a video game generally have as good a time as those who have played for a while. The difference is that the more experienced players know how to get much more mileage out of a quarter. You can usually spot a new player by how fast he pumps quarters into the machine.

Putting quarters into the machine is like putting your karmic token on the line for your life experiences. You don't know much about the game, so naturally you make mistakes. Some people will become so impatient with their mistakes that they'll get tired of that game. Instead of trying to improve at it, they'll jump from one game to another. They are like the spiritual shopper.

The spiritual shopper jumps from one spiritual path to another, never getting very good at any of them, never really able to find truth in any of them. A person like this might find he is better off to just stay in one religion and get all the experience that he can out of it. By jumping from path to path, he often creates more karma for himself, and he really does not move very far forward in his spiritual unfoldment. Most people do not realize this.

The Initiate Report

I received a monthly initiate report from an ECKist. Actually a letter from the ECK initiate to me, the purpose of the report is to give the person an overview of the spiritual progress he has made—or not made—over the past month. He tries to assess not only what he has learned since the last report, but what he still needs to learn. These letters often describe the events that surround the spiritual principle he has been working with.

In this letter, the initiate said that he had become very disgruntled over something another ECKist was doing. He had let the man know how he felt about it. But over the next few weeks, the incident continued to bother him. Had he done the right thing by speaking up?

One night in contemplation, the ECKist had an experience. The Inner Master came to him and asked, "What do you always tell people when you give introductory presentations?"

"I tell them a lot of things," the ECKist mumbled, not sure what this was all about.

The Master clarified the question: "But what do you always say at the end of each one?"

"I tell them that the greatest love I can give to others is to grant them the space to be themselves."

"Have you done this with your brother?" the Inner Master asked.

The Greatest Love

The ECKist knew immediately what the Master was referring to. He got the message: the greatest love gives others the space to be themselves.

The spiritual philosophy flowed easily when he was presenting it to others in a relatively benign situation, such as an ECK introductory presentation. But when the time came to employ the principle in his everyday life, he hadn't found it quite so easy. The other ECKist had gotten under his skin.

Mentally reviewing the incident that had perturbed him so much, he realized that he had interfered in something that was none of his business. It concerned the other man's personal life. The ECKist knew he had been out of line to judge another person's actions; he had no right to do this. Rather than concern himself with what others did, he would be better off to keep his own karmic balance in order.

As he pondered this realization, his wife came into the room. She had just finished bringing their monthly finances up to date.

"Are you ready for some good news?" she said.

"What is it?" he asked. He was curious to find out why her face was all lit up.

"I made a mistake last month," she said happily. "We have six hundred dollars more in our bank account than I thought."

The ECKist recognized this as outer verification of a truth he had just gotten on the inner: Be careful to keep your own life in balance, and you will benefit spiritually. Though the message manifested as a financial bonus out here, he could see the spiritual connection.

The greatest love we can give is to allow other people

to be themselves. Therefore, we never impose the ECK teachings on anyone who does not want to hear them. But when the ECK, or Holy Spirit, opens up a conversation and a truth seeker asks, "What can I find out about ECK? What can it do for me?" it's all right to go ahead and talk about it. Because if you withhold truth from people who ask for it, then how will truth ever be passed along?

Dream Guidance

Many ECK initiates are given guidance through the dream state. A situation may be mocked up by the Dream Master to simulate something that is causing the ECKist concern in his daily life. Through this dream, the ECKist is shown what he should or should not be doing if he wants to resolve the situation.

The ECK dream discourses can help you learn to work more effectively with the dream state. Many books on dreams rely on a specific list of symbols. They would have you believe that symbols like a pebble or a vulture mean the same thing for everybody. But it is unlikely that you will get your own truth out of someone else's interpretations. For this reason, I use symbols only as a way to show you how to interpret your own.

The dream discourses discuss the structure of dreams and how they relate to your everyday life in the physical world. More importantly, they show you how to make the connection between your inner life and your outer life. Bringing the unknown inner part of yourself to your outer consciousness can help you make your life better in every way, for your own spiritual good.

The discourses include spiritual techniques. These are used step-by-step, month-by-month to break up the ingrained thought patterns which are holding you back.

The Call of Soul

People often spend their whole lives looking for ECK. They become spiritual shoppers, going from one religion to another. Though they might be better off to focus their full attention on one religion in this lifetime, that may not be possible.

If, on the other hand, you are a sincere seeker of truth, you realize that something within is constantly pushing you. You know the answers you seek are somewhere in the world. This inner force that pushes you to find them is an urge that you have no control over. It is the call of Soul.

Soul is experiencing the music of God, which can be heard as Sound or seen as Light. It is an unconscious inner experience which the outer, or human, side of the individual is not aware of. Outwardly, all he knows is this gnawing feeling that there is more to life than he can learn in his present religion. So he begins his search through different philosophies, looking for the missing link.

Renewing Your Search

An ECK initiate was on a flight to Perth, Australia. Seated beside him was a woman who was returning home to Perth after a visit with relatives in Canada. "This was my last trip to Canada," she told him. "I'm in my seventies now."

When the woman found out that the ECKist had never been to Perth, she was delighted to answer his questions about the climate, culture, and things to do.

"What are you reading?" she inquired, glancing at the book in his hand.

"It's called *Soul Travelers of the Far Country*," he said. "It is written by the spiritual leader of ECKANKAR, the Living ECK Master. It's about Soul's journey through this world."

The woman mentioned a number of spiritual paths that she had joined at one time or another. "I was always looking for a certain element of truth, but I never found it," she said sadly. "Finally, I just gave up and quit all religions. I came to the conclusion that this day-to-day existence is all I can expect from life. Now I'm just putting in my time until it's over."

Yet she was curious about ECKANKAR and started asking some questions.

The ECKist explained that the teachings of ECK are based on the Light and Sound. He also told her about HU, the sacred name for God, which we often sing during our spiritual exercises. "The reason I'm going to Perth is to attend an ECKANKAR seminar," he said.

The woman was interested, but at this point in her life she felt she was too old to renew her search.

"Soul has no age," the ECKist said. "It doesn't matter when you begin to look for truth. It's beyond age and time. It makes no difference whether you would have found it in your teens, or whether you find it now in your seventies. Truth is ever new. When you are ready, it will find you."

His words made sense to her. All of a sudden she was struck by the timing of the situation. On a flight back from what was to be her last trip to Canada, she had found herself seated next to this ECKist. He was going to a seminar in her hometown of Perth, of all places. It occurred to her how fully and completely this ECK works. She was grateful to finally have heard about It.

Waiting for Truth

Another ECKist went sightseeing with a group of friends in London. While admiring the architecture of Westminster Abbey, he happened to notice a bag lady. One of those impoverished people who live on the streets, she was seated outside the abbey on a bench.

This woman was unusual in that she had a full, yellowish-white, silken beard. He wanted to get a picture of her as a souvenir, but he didn't know quite how to go about it without insulting her.

When she looked the other way, he moved within a few feet of her and quickly snapped the picture. To his surprise, she turned her head and looked right at him, then she beckoned him over.

"You're just like all the other tourists, aren't you?" she said.

"No," he said.

"Why not?" she asked. "How are you so different?"

He thought for a moment before answering. "Because I'm here to try to understand why the other religions have lost the Light and Sound," he finally said. He then mentioned that he was in London to attend an ECKANKAR seminar.

As he told her a little bit about ECK, he saw her eyes light up with interest. She said, "I have been coming to Westminster Abbey to sit on this bench every day for the last thirty years. Every day I have asked God for guidance. I just knew that this would be the place where my answer would come." Somewhere along the way, she said, she had given up everything and began living on streets. So he told her about chanting HU to raise oneself in consciousness.

Then she asked him, "Can I have a copy of the picture you took?"

"Sure," he said. "Where can I send it to you when I get home?"

Then she said, "On second thought, you don't have to bother sending that picture to me."

This comment worried him. Why had she changed her mind? Was this her way of saying that she wouldn't be around to receive the picture? That she was going to try for instant heavenly bliss by doing something silly, like taking her own life?

In ECK we realize that you can't take shortcuts. You have to see life through. The life you are living now is the one you have made for yourself in past lives. If you can't meet the problems this time, you will have to come back again and face the same ones, magnified many more times. You will keep doing this until you finally come to recognize that you cannot run away from yourself.

The ECKist cautiously questioned the woman as to why she didn't want him to send the picture. As she talked, he became convinced that she was not contemplating suicide. She was simply trying to tell him that she would no longer be spending her days on that bench, and she didn't need a reminder of it. He had told her what she had been waiting all these years to hear. She had no reason to come back again; it was time to move on. Now that she knew about HU, she had what she needed to take her the next step on the path to God.

Golden Moments

Often the greatest love you can give another is just to be yourself. Be alert for that golden moment when the Holy Spirit brings you to someone who wants to hear about ECK.

You don't have to preach a sermon. Usually you only need to introduce them to the two aspects of the Holy Spirit, the Sound and Light. If they want to know how to reach the Sound and Light themselves, explain that the best way is through chanting HU for fifteen or twenty minutes a day.

Master Power

I always recommend that people do their spiritual exercises every day. But they should be done with a sense of excitement and anticipation. Look for that friend of all friends—the Mahanta—who resides within you. This is the Master Power. It is the power of love.

This kind of power has nothing to do with one-upmanship or competition. The power of love is the spiritual consciousness that makes its appearance within you. It is the part of ECK we call the Inner Master.

In ECK we recognize the two sides of the Master—the Outer and the Inner Master. This coincides with the outer and inner teachings. We know that the outer sounds and lights, which are manifestations of the ECK, or Holy Spirit, on the physical plane, also have their counterparts of Light and Sound on the inner planes. The farther you go into the inner worlds, into the Far Country, the purer, higher, and more refined the Light and Sound become.

The Right Wave

An ECKist visiting Hawaii went swimming one day. After almost four hours in the water, he decided to borrow a short surfboard and learn to ride the waves.

The board was about the length of his torso, and he lay on the board in the water and paddled around to get the feel of it. He was about to try riding the next wave, when he heard the voice of the Inner Master. It was telling him, "Don't take this wave."

This didn't make any sense. He wanted to learn how to surf, it was a great wave, and his mind told him to grab it while he could.

But the Inner Master said, "Don't take this wave."

He watched the wave go by. Then he noticed two young men struggling farther out in the ocean. They had the same type of short surfboards that he had. The huge wave had torn the surfboard out from under one of them, and he seemed to be in trouble.

The ECKist paddled his board in their direction to see if he could help. The two surfers had gotten back together, and they were both clinging to the remaining board. The ECKist didn't really want to interfere as long as they were doing all right. But he hovered nearby, just in case.

Another huge wave crashed over the two surfers and separated them. When the wave settled, the ECKist saw that the one who had lost his grip on the board was thrashing about in the water. He looked about twenty years old. "I think I'm in trouble," he shouted, gasping for breath. "Can you help?"

"Don't worry, we'll get you back," the ECKist reassured him. But now he noticed that the waves had carried them farther out into the ocean. The people back at the shore looked like little ants. We're both in trouble, he thought.

"Grab my board and hang on," he shouted, grasping the swimmer's wrist.

"Don't let go of me," the young man pleaded, and the ECKist now saw the first gleam of panic in his eyes.

"Don't worry, I've got you," he said.

With one hand on his board and the other holding the swimmer's wrist, the ECK initiate began to kick his way back to shore. They were able to catch a couple of waves, and soon they were in shallow waters.

An older man ran out to meet them. "Is my son OK?" he asked worriedly. The ECKist assured him that his son was fine.

"My other boy is still out there," the father said. The second surfer was the young man's fourteen-year-old brother. Neither of them was an experienced surfer.

In the meantime, another ECKist had paddled his board to the struggling boy. But they were pretty far out, and both seemed to be having a problem.

The ECK initiate was exhausted from over four hours of swimming and surfing, but he took his board back into the water and went out to help them.

The fourteen-year-old boy was ashen gray from fear and exhaustion. The two ECKists pulled him onto one of their boards and positioned him in the center. "Hang on!" they instructed him. With an ECKist on either side, the boy hung on to the board, and they made their way back to shore.

The two ECKists delivered the second son to his father. To avoid the crowd that had gathered, they immediately went back into the water. They weren't looking for any attention. The two young men's lives had been saved— that was all that mattered. The ECKists stayed in the water until the crowd had dispersed then quietly went back to their hotel.

On the Verge of Eternity

Talking about truth is sometimes pretty easy. The greatest love is not just a willingness to share truth with another. In this case, the greatest love was expressed by the ECK initiate's willingness to put his very life on the line for someone else.

"The faces of those two young men will be imprinted on my mind forever," the ECKist said. In the struggle between life and death, Soul was at the forefront. All social pretensions were washed away. Soul looked out and said, "Here we are on the verge of eternity again."

The ECKist realized that it was the Mahanta who had made it possible for him to save the two young men. When the Inner Master said, "Don't take this wave," he had listened.

This story illustrates why it is so important for the ECK initiates to integrate their inner and outer lives. Only then can one begin to become a clear channel for the Holy Spirit, the divine ECK. This is what I am trying to accomplish through the talks, books, and discourses. Their purpose is to show you how you can open yourself to your full potential as a spiritual being, and eventually as a spiritual giant.

Being a spiritual giant does not mean you will be in a position to lord your mastery over other people. You evolve into a spiritual giant in the sense that you become the greatest servant for all you meet. And being the greatest servant, you will also have the greatest love.

Show Me Love

After the World Wide of ECK in Houston, an initiate wanted to share her experiences with another ECKist. One Sunday they got together and went for a walk in a beautiful forest. As they walked the ECKist began to tell her friend about all the love she had experienced at the seminar.

They came to a clearing and found themselves on top of a cliff that rose out of the forest. A clear lake sparkled below; overhead, the sky was a brilliant blue. What a perfect day, the ECKist thought.

Turning to her friend she said, "In one of the workshops at the seminar, we were told that if we wanted to find divine love, we could chant HU quietly within ourselves. At the same time we could say: 'Show me love, Mahanta. Show me love, Mahanta.' This seems like a perfect time to do it."

And so, standing high atop a cliff overlooking the sparkling blue lake, the ECKist began to chant HU. "Show me love, Mahanta," she said silently. "Show me love, Mahanta."

All of a sudden a small flock of birds came fluttering down. Some landed on the ground in front of her while others perched in a nearby tree.

The Inner Master nudged the chela, "Hold out your hand." She felt silly, but she put out her hand. One little bird flew down from the tree and lit on it.

"This can't be," she said, laughing with joy. She felt the love of the ECK and the Mahanta coming through the little bird. The love was so strong and pure that she began to weep. She realized the ECK cared so much for her that It would show her Its love even through the humblest of Its creatures.

They left the cliff and continued on their walk. About two hours later, they came back the same way. "I'm going to try it again," she said.

Silently she chanted HU and said, "Show me love, Mahanta. Show me love." She almost couldn't believe it: another flock of birds flew down, she held out her hand, and once again, a little bird landed on it.

She knew then that the love of the ECK is real; that the love of the ECK is truth. It is Light and Sound, and It will show Itself through the humblest of Its creatures — if only we will be the humblest of Its creatures.

Hawaiian Regional Seminar, Honolulu, Hawaii,
November 21, 1987

He was in the temple of his own consciousness. Sometimes that can be a small, mean, dark place. What we try to accomplish in ECK is to open up this temple, to make it a big, bright, happy place filled with pretty flowers and gaily colored butterflies.

5

In Our Own Temple

ECKists who give the talks and conduct workshops and roundtable forums at the ECK seminars make it look so easy. They seem so relaxed. Many people think they do this sort of thing all the time. But it's not so. Most of them are shaking in their boots.

Opening to ECK

Two High Initiates were asked to conduct a workshop. Usually the workshop facilitators talk in the months preceding a seminar and plan their program. They work out a rough agenda of what they are going to present to the attendees and submit it to Seminar Services for review. But for one reason or another, these two H.I.'s were unable to get together more than once or twice.

They tried to set aside some additional preparation time when they arrived at the seminar, but they were both so busy with meetings and volunteer activities that it couldn't be arranged.

The workshop was to begin in twenty minutes, and the woman and her partner had not yet had enough time to prepare. The room was filled to capacity—about two hundred people. She couldn't help wondering how they were going to handle it.

Her concern grew even more when her partner walked in and said, "There's another meeting that I have to attend, so I'll have to leave halfway through the workshop." Oh, great, she thought. "But don't worry about it," he added. "I'll get things started with a spiritual exercise."

He led the audience through the exercise. When it was over, he asked for comments and questions while she dutifully carried the microphone around the room. She was beginning to feel quite comfortable about the way it was going, when suddenly he said, "I have to leave now."

The woman stood there listening to the click, click, click of his footsteps as he walked down the long aisle to the door at the back of the room. The door clanged shut behind him, and then there was silence. I'm here all alone, she thought.

Anyone who has ever been through a similar experience knows the feeling: sheer terror.

An interesting thing happened then. With nothing or no one else to lean on, she opened herself completely to the ECK. And the ECK came flowing through. Soon the workshop was over, and the crowd headed out the door.

Several people came up to her in the hall. "That was the most wonderful workshop I have ever been to," one person said. "The love of the ECK was so strong."

Another said, "When your partner left and the door slammed shut, I felt so sorry for you. If I had been in your place, I couldn't have done it." Then she added, "But for the first time, I got to see the transformation that takes place when the ECK is working in a person. You became totally different."

Inner Stretching

It is here in our own consciousness, our own temple of spiritual learning, that the Mahanta finds one means or another to stretch us. He is always pulling us a little bit farther than we've ever gone before. The more active we become for ECK, the more it seems our best plans are pushed aside. Sometimes it even seems as though other people are devising schemes to make our life as difficult as possible.

How am I going to take this next step for ECK? we wonder. But something always happens. If you trust totally in the ECK and do the best you can, then whatever you do will be exactly as it is supposed to be.

A Little Planning

Another Higher Initiate found himself in a similar spot when he was asked to speak at a seminar. It was his understanding that he was to give one talk. But when he arrived at the seminar, the program director told him, "We've got you scheduled for two talks."

"Two talks?" he said.

"Yes. And we also scheduled you to lead a workshop, the teen session, and a couple of other activities. As you can see, your name has already been printed on the program in several places."

"This is way too much," the Higher Initiate said. "I need time to prepare before I go out and speak to people about ECK. I know I could trust in the ECK, but I like to do a little planning too. This schedule doesn't give me a chance to do it."

"Well, I guess we can take you off some of these things," the program director said.

"I'll go ahead and do it this time," the Higher Initiate said. "But let's keep to our original agreement from now on. If there are any changes, let me know in advance."

As it turned out, this misunderstanding served a double purpose. The first one was to stretch this individual beyond his usual capacity. Everyone has his limits, of course, and in this case he felt he had reached them. But they will remain limits only until he has a chance to accept and adapt to his new level of capability.

The second benefit to arise from this incident came when the man led a workshop for other Higher Initiates. Using his own experience as an example, he was able to advance the need for greater understanding and respect among the ECK initiates. In other words, treat each other as you would like to be treated. Think how you would feel, for instance, if you showed up at a seminar prepared to give one talk, and discovered that you were expected to give three or four or five. It can be frightening. I know, because it has happened to me in the past.

Lesson in Humility

Last night my wife and I went out to dinner with a couple of friends. We were anxious to try out a restaurant where the food was reputed to be very good. Besides that, we had coupons for a 20 percent discount.

I tried to dress casually, but my wife said to wear a suit coat. It's just as well I did. It was one of those snooty places with a dim, candlelight atmosphere and a different waiter for every function. But that didn't stop our group from ambling in the door in our informal, erratic fashion.

The maître d' led us to a booth set for two. I sat down and slid over to the wall. The waiter in charge of setting our table rushed over with additional napkins and utensils. I quickly grabbed one of the place settings that was already on the table and started to move it over in front of me. This way, I figured, he wouldn't have to reach so far.

"*I* will do that," he said, practically snatching the stuff out of my hand.

The waiter who brought our menus was every bit as pompous and haughty as the first one. Uh-oh, I thought. That usually means high prices and a skimpy selection of food.

As soon as I flipped open the menu, my suspicions were confirmed. Nothing really appealed to me. I thought about suggesting that we leave, but it was too late to look for another restaurant. I wanted to get some rest and get up early enough to prepare for this morning's talk. It was easier to just pick something.

Despite all that, our group was having a pretty good time. The waiter who finally came to take our orders didn't look pleased about that at all. Maybe he wasn't used to seeing happy people in this establishment.

When my wife asked about different items on the menu, he made it a point to answer her questions in his most condescending manner. I guess he wanted to make sure we knew we were in a very fine restaurant. He had no way of knowing, of course, that the ECK works in Its own ways to bring humility to those who need it.

I noticed one of the women in our group squinting in the dim light at something behind my wife. "There's a cockroach crawling on the back of the seat," she whispered to me. Fortunately, my wife was leaning forward, still talking to the waiter.

Three of us kept our eyes fastened on the bug. The waiter finally looked up, then turned to see what we were all staring at. Spotting the roach, some of his haughtiness disappeared. He grabbed a cloth napkin and made a grand, sweeping gesture over the place where the roach had been crawling around. "Ah-ha!" he said triumphantly. "I have him!"

But he didn't. The bug had managed to scoot away.

Continuing with his charade, the waiter flung the napkin to the floor and stomped on it. Then he picked it up and neatly tucked it in the bottom of a tray of dirty dishes. "You have to expect these things when you're in Hawaii," was all he said by way of an apology.

The man was almost humble as he took our orders. And he stayed that way until it came time to tally up the bill, which was much lower than he was accustomed to. With those prices, we had all decided to skip the appetizers and dessert. That may have been a mistake, though. Each meal was served on a fancy oval plate with a generous portion of rice arranged around the edges. Planted in the center was the dab of meat that passed for the main course. It looked OK at first glance, but closer inspection revealed that there wasn't too much going on inside the border of rice.

My wife looked over the bill. "This doesn't tally right," she said to our waiter.

"It certainly does," he insisted, his snootiness returning. He started to recheck the figures, unaware that his arm was only an inch above one of the candles. I clutched a glass of ice water, just in case his coat suddenly went up in smoke. But he backed off in time, and I didn't get to play hero.

He also discovered that he had overcharged us by two dollars.

The ECK does things like this to all of us. These incidents keep us humble and therefore more open to life. They force us to put aside our pretensions so that we can recognize that the people around us are no less important than we are.

Your Temple of Consciousness

The waiter didn't have the awareness to realize that we are all Soul; that each of us—including the little bug—had come to that room to have our own experiences. He needed to be shown that he wasn't higher or better than the customers.

He was in the temple of his own consciousness. Sometimes that can be a small, mean, dark place. What we try to accomplish in ECK is to open up this temple, to make it a big, bright, happy place filled with pretty flowers and gaily colored butterflies.

Moving Forward

Reports that describe success with the Shariyat technique are especially fitting for this First Year of the Shariyat. One came in recently from a couple who were trying to buy a house. At one point, negotiations with the sellers and their agent got so bogged down that the transaction came to a standstill. In the meantime, they were forced to live in temporary quarters, which caused them even more stress.

One day the wife said to herself, "I think I'll do the Shariyat technique. I'll give it just one try."

First she stated her question: How can we move forward with these negotiations? Then she opened *The Shariyat-Ki-Sugmad* at random, hoping the Golden-tongued Wisdom would give her more insight into the situation.

The first sentence she read didn't seem to apply to her question at all. No matter how she stretched her

81

imagination, she couldn't relate it to the problem of trying to close the deal on this house. She read a little further along but still found no connection. Finally she gave up.

When her husband got home that evening, she told him about her attempt to use the Shariyat technique. "The passage I read just didn't seem to relate to my question," she said. Noticing his expression, she asked, "Why do you look so surprised?"

"The same thing happened to me," he said. "I asked how we could get through the negotiations and get moved in. Then I opened *The Shariyat,* and the passage I read didn't make any sense to me, either."

Now it was the wife's turn to be surprised, because his question had been the same as hers. When he mentioned the first sentence he had read when he randomly opened *The Shariyat,* they discovered it was the very same one she had read.

"Maybe we should go over that passage one more time," he suggested, reaching for the book.

The sentence they read again was this: "The Atma— Soul—is a neuter atom of the Divine Source of life." They talked it over, trying to figure out how it applied to the closing on the house.

"The key must be in the fact that Soul is a neuter atom," they concluded. "Maybe that means we should stay in a neutral state, instead of getting so upset every time we disagree with the sellers."

From that point on, they went through the negotiations not caring whether they got the house or not. This detachment actually strengthened their position in the bargaining process. Whenever the sellers and their agent raised the issues that had caused such an emotional reaction before, the couple merely looked at them and said, quite calmly, "That isn't acceptable."

Soon after that, the parties came to terms which were agreeable and beneficial to both sides, and the couple moved into their new home.

This is just one example of how ECKists are using the Shariyat technique to help them resolve problems. Many people have found it to be a wonderful technique.

Facing Yourself

In our own temple, we sometimes come face to face with ourselves. This includes facing the fears and other useless things that have become part of us, but which we no longer need.

A Third Initiate had an inner experience in which he went to an ancient, dark, gloomy temple. Two monks in dark brown robes solemnly stood guard at the entrance. "Come in," they said as he walked up to them.

Before going inside, he decided to test them. "Are you of the SUGMAD?" he asked.

"Yes," they said, "we are of the SUGMAD."

That's the right answer, he thought—but something doesn't feel right. Nervously he questioned them again: "Are you of the Mahanta?" As he waited for their reply, the two monks disappeared.

In ECK we learn to question the forms that appear on the inner planes. An inner nudge generally tells you when something is wrong. If you meet beings who claim to represent the SUGMAD, the ECK, the Mahanta, or the Vairagi Order, and it doesn't feel right, then challenge them. You may have to do it two or three times, but eventually the forms will lose their force.

Farther along in ECK, you realize that the entities you meet on the inner planes are not from some strange source outside of you; they are of your own creation.

The ECKist now saw two empty robes in the spot where the two priests had been standing. The bodies were gone. He struck the robes with a stick and watched them fall to the stone floor.

He knew then that these were nothing more than forms he had created in the past with his thoughts and fears. They disappeared because they were no longer of any use to him, and no longer stood in the way of his spiritual unfoldment.

Transforming the Temple

In contemplation sometime after that, he found that he was able to come back to the very same temple. This time he went inside.

What a dark, dreary place, he thought. I'm going to lighten it up.

He removed some stones from the wall, and sunlight came pouring in. Then he went outside and planted a flower garden. As he looked around at the changes he had made, he now saw beauty.

He was able to do this because he was in the temple of his own consciousness. In this case, it was located on the Causal Plane, the level to which his Third Initiation took him. Here he found the karmic cause of everything that he had created for himself.

Indeed, as we begin the journey through the ECK initiations, we often find that the temple in which we reside is dark and dreary. But as we go higher, as our consciousness expands, the useless thought forms disappear. Living things start to come in, and the temple becomes a brighter, more beautiful place.

Through the study of ECK and the practice of the spiritual exercises, we transform the temple of our

84

consciousness. This is what he was doing, and this is what you can do.

Struck by Lightning

There are many dimensions to the ways in which the Mahanta works with an individual. One afternoon a woman and her son were at home during a severe thunderstorm. All of a sudden lightning struck the house, traveled down through the wiring in the chandelier, and lit up the entire living room. A loud clap of thunder followed close behind it.

The son, who was in the room where the lightning entered, saw a purplish blue light of electricity buzz all around him. Streams of electricity flowed from his fingers to the wall socket. All he could do was stand there motionless as this current poured through him.

His mother saw the room transformed into tiny atoms of golden light, like stardust. It was sparkling all over.

As soon as the lightning flash was gone, a column of light came down through the center of the room from ceiling to floor. As the woman and her son watched, the Mahanta appeared in this pillar of light, and with him were a number of other ECK Masters. Silently they left the light and sat down at the dining-room table, where they began to talk with the mother and son. After a while, they walked back into the column of light and went away.

Nothing in the home had been damaged by the lightning. There were no burned spots anywhere, the chandelier was intact, and even the delicate little bulbs within it were in good condition.

The column of light was visible to the woman for quite a few days after that. The next time she and her son sat down for a half-hour HU Chant, the Mahanta and other ECK Masters appeared again. This time they sat around a crystal table unlike any she had in her home. She was seeing on the inner planes now, where she was able to watch them as they worked on a manuscript of the Shariyat-Ki-Sugmad.

This went on for some time, then gradually, over a period of several months, the column of light began to dim.

The light she saw was actually a ray that started from the highest planes. It came down through the spiritual worlds and entered the lower worlds as a beam of light.

Both mother and son recognized that they'd had the protection of the Mahanta during the storm. At the same time, the experience was used to open their consciousness. This enabled them to see the Masters at work on the inner planes and even speak with them for a while.

This is the kind of experience that comes to initiates who are pure of heart. With their whole being they love the SUGMAD, the ECK, and the Mahanta—without reservation, without criticism, without limitation.

I don't often share letters that come in from ECKists, but sometimes it is important to put them on record. As I recount their experiences, they become part of ECK history. It is a way of forming the Shariyat-Ki-Sugmad, the ever-growing scriptures of ECK.

A Meeting with Rebazar Tarzs

An ECK initiate wrote to me about her first meeting with Rebazar Tarzs, which took place when she was in the first grade. She is well aware that some people question the existence of the ECK Masters. They are quick to assume that Rebazar Tarzs, Fubbi Quantz, and the others whose names appear in the ECK works must have been figments of Paul Twitchell's imagination. Yet, this woman was having experiences with these ECK Masters in the early 1930s, some thirty years before Paul brought out the teachings.

Her letter also helps to explain some of the nightmares that children and adults have—and what they can do about them. People who ask me for help in ridding themselves of nightmares do not realize that what the ECK Masters want to do is to teach you how to face your own fears.

Nightmares are simply your own fears, manifested on the inner planes. As long as you are overcome by fear, you are never really free; and you will never have freedom until you learn how to face yourself.

The whole point of ECKANKAR is to teach the individual how to reach spiritual freedom and to go back to God in this lifetime, by way of the Light and Sound. In ECK this education is carried out through the Mahanta and through the assistance of the ECK Masters.

Her letter read:

Dear Harji,

Every now and then we read or hear that someone is questioning the existence of the Masters of the Vairagi. But Rebazar Tarzs started teaching and guiding me when I was in the first grade. This was in the early 1930s.

My first recall of him was a series of dreams that are still as vivid now as when they were occurring. One night I found myself in a long underground tunnel. I knew there were bodies buried in the walls. At intervals there were candles burning in niches.

I heard growling and snarling behind me and turned to see a pack of vicious-looking wolves coming toward me. I turned and ran.

Being chased by creatures is a nightmare many children have. They don't realize, of course, where the creatures come from or what to do about it. The letter goes on to say:

I ran until I was so tired, but they were still behind me. I called out for help, and I heard, "Turn around and face them." I kept on running and shortly came awake.

The next night I found myself in the same place, and the wolves were still chasing me. After a while they sounded closer, and I turned to find they had gained on me.

I called out for help and saw two men. One was dark and wore a reddish-brown robe. [Later she identifies him as Rebazar Tarzs.] The other was lighter in coloring, dressed in white with a white beard. [Though she never identifies him, this was Fubbi Quantz.]

I ran toward them, but they receded in front of me. I called again for help, and the dark man said, "Turn around and face them." I thought, I've already looked at them twice—and kept on running. Soon I found myself awake again.

This went on for two more nights. I didn't ask for any more help. I just managed to stay ahead of the wolves.

On the fifth night, once again I found myself in the same situation, but this time I passed one of the candles and noticed that it flickered. So did the next one. I looked up to see that they were almost used up. Each candle I passed was the same way.

I knew I could not negotiate the rough ground and the turns in the dark. Once again I called for help, and once again the two men were there in the distance. Once again the dark man with the beard repeated, "Turn around and face them."

The thought that came was, If I'm going to die, I would rather do it in the light than in the dark. I stopped and turned to face the wolves. I looked at them for a few seconds, then they disappeared. The men who had been in the distance were now standing beside me with their hands on my shoulders, smiling at me. And then I awoke.

The next night, I found myself above ground, standing at the beginning of a long lane with trees growing on both sides. At the end of the lane was a big house with a door. The top of the door was stained glass. It had all the symbols of the different religions. There was the six-pointed star, the cross, the crescent moon, and others. There was a bright light shining behind the door. I didn't know how, but I knew what each symbol meant.

I started to walk down the lane. A priest in a black cassock came out from behind a tree and told me to turn back, the place was evil. As I stood there, I heard another voice urge me on. I recognized the voice from the tunnel with the wolves and turned. It was the dark, bearded man in the maroon robe. Where I had felt fear and danger from the priest, I felt strength, kindness, and love from the bearded man. I continued to walk toward the door then found myself awake in bed.

The next night, I was on the lane where I had left off. Once again the priest was trying to frighten me into turning back with threats of death and hell. The man in the maroon robe urged me on with love and kindness. My trust was with the bearded man with the beautiful eyes and the good strength. I walked on.

This went on for two more days until, on the fifth day, I found myself at the foot of the steps leading to the door. The priest said that if I went up and opened the door, I would burn in hell forever. The bearded man urged me to have no fear and to open the door.

I walked up the stairs and opened the door. Instead of a room on the other side, there was brilliant, white, loving light and such beautiful music. Once again, the bearded man was beside me with his hand on my shoulder. We walked into the light, then I found myself awake in bed again.

Here she switches to her outer life:

Some weeks later, I started catechism class in preparation for first communion. The nuns and the priest would often say that if someone was not a Catholic, they could never go to heaven. Each time, I was reminded inwardly of the door and what I had found behind it. That treasured friend and teacher was there to help me in the inner world of dreams and on the outer.

Then she refers to occasions where Rebazar Tarzs helped her in her outer life. Some of them are quite dramatic, though she doesn't go into great detail.

One day on the outer, he helped me save my parents from two men who had come to kill them. Another time I had just learned to swim a little that day. He talked me through so that I was able to save my cousin from drowning.

It wasn't until my sophomore year in high school, 1940–41, that I finally brought his name back from the dream state. It was Rebazar Tarzs.

I had been studying with both Jesus and Rebazar for many years. One day Jesus said—three times—that I must learn to die and that I would be studying with Rebazar.

Saint Paul referred to this in the Bible when he spoke of dying daily. That means learning to rise above the human consciousness into the spiritual consciousness. To do this, we must leave the concerns of our daily life behind for a little while every day. There is no other way to go into the high states of Spirit.

The letter goes on to say:

The next night I found myself with Rebazar again. He said that Jesus taught up to this region, but it was time to go on into other regions. Then he said, "Bless you in the name of the SUGMAD," and kissed me over the Spiritual Eye.

90

The next night I sought out Jesus and asked about what Rebazar had said. He repeated the same thing, blessed me in the same fashion, and said, "Now return to your Master." I did, and there I stayed.

In 1970, she finally read her first book by Paul Twitchell, *ECKANKAR—The Key to Secret Worlds.* Not only was she surprised to run across the name *Rebazar Tarzs,* but to learn that Paul had met him, too.

She then expressed her gratitude to the Mahanta, Rebazar, Paul, and the other Masters of the Vairagi. "My life has been so enriched by you all. Thank you," she said in closing.

An Ongoing Spiritual Exercise

I would like to suggest a simple spiritual exercise that you can do throughout the First Year of the Shariyat. Each month, read a chapter of *The Shariyat-Ki-Sugmad,* Book One. Do it at your leisure. You can read a few sentences or a couple of paragraphs at a time. Pay particular attention to the chapter title. How does the chapter relate to the title? And how does it all relate back to you?

You can use this as an ongoing, casual spiritual exercise. It is a way to spiritualize yourself, to keep close to the Mahanta, the ECK, and the SUGMAD.

The ECK seminars are followed by so many reports from people who found upliftment and spiritual help, both during and after the seminar. I think you'll find the same is true of this one. You need only walk through the door of your own temple.

May the blessings be.

Hawaiian Regional Seminar, Honolulu, Hawaii,
Sunday, November 22, 1987

The kangaroos symbolized the springiness of Soul—
happy, bouncing, always jumping around.

6

Feed My Kangaroos

On any spiritual path, you find people with the tendency to get so involved and so zealous that they lose their balance. They take life so seriously that they forget to see the humor and the enjoyment in the little things.

This is a stage that Soul goes through on Its path. It doesn't happen to everyone, but it can happen to certain people in any religion.

In ECK, when we become pious and self-righteous about our path, we sometimes close off the spiritual flow that comes through to make our life better. How can we communicate or be of service to others as a channel for the Holy Spirit when we are so caught up in ourselves?

Maybe we can't help being enthusiastic about the teachings, but we never want to approach others with such missionary zeal that we deny them the same spiritual freedom we want for ourselves.

Spiritual Bonds

Americans have an interesting bond with Australians. Many of our respective ancestors, whom we boastfully refer to as blue bloods, were actually convicted criminals banished from England. America was the main dumping ground for a while, but after the American War of Independence, England established a convict colony in Australia. Since both of our countries were populated by the unwanted children of our common mother country, I guess you could say we're related.

The closer relationship, of course, is that we are spiritual brothers and sisters in ECK. The teachings of ECK are about the Light and Sound of the Holy Spirit. The ECK is the Voice of God that comes down through the many different heavens into the lower worlds, including earth.

Aspects of God's Voice

The Voice of God is not something that speaks to us in a commanding, booming voice from the clouds. It doesn't give orders or say, "Ah, my son, my daughter, you must do this or that, and I shall be pleased with thee evermore." It doesn't work that way. The Voice of God is known to us through Its two aspects, the Light and Sound.

The Light can be seen as any number of different colors—blue, white, yellow, green, lavender, purple, pink, or even in combinations of golden-green, bluish white, and so on. Some people have an experience with the Light even before they come to ECK. They tend to see these colors during a significant event in their life—when they are ill, lonely, afraid, or feel that life has forsaken them. The experience generally has an uplifting or soothing effect on them; and not knowing its source, they may spend many years trying to find an explanation.

The Light is usually the first aspect of the ECK, or Holy Spirit, that an individual will encounter, but not always. Sometimes the Voice of God first makes Itself

94

known through the Sound. One of the classic forms of the Sound is the single note of a flute. A number of people have mentioned that they suddenly heard the sound of a flute during a HU Chant. It was so clear and distinct that they thought it was being played by someone in the room.

This is the Sound from the other planes. It is the Voice of God speaking directly to Soul rather than to the mind. Only the lower deities, the lower manifestations of God, speak in words.

The Snoring Chela

The other day I was very concerned about the spiritual welfare of an individual. I was making some notes about the situation, when all of a sudden I heard the sound of a man breathing heavily, almost on the verge of a snore.

My wife and I were working in the same room at the time; she was at a desk about four feet from mine. Our doors and windows were locked, so it was unlikely anyone could have gotten in. Still, I went and looked in the closet. "There's nobody in there," my wife said. I knew that, but it was so loud that I had to check it out for my mind's sake.

I realized I was listening to this person in his spiritual state. He was asleep spiritually. It confirmed what I needed to know and do.

Many times people feel that the Living ECK Master is unaware of a situation because he won't act for a while. "Doesn't he know what's happening?" they say. "Doesn't he know this person is doing these terrible things, causing me such discomfort, and making my life miserable? When will he do something about it?"

All I can say is: Be patient. Help is coming eventually. In the meantime, whether you recognize it or not, things are being worked out. While these situations are coming to a head, so much karma is worked out. The parties involved in the confrontation are lightened of the load. They have released their attachment to the situation, to their self-esteem, and to any of the other vain, petty things that the mind considers so important.

Pure Heart

So many things seem so important to us—our opinions, our religion. We are all too willing to fight or hate somebody over them. We're willing to do all sorts of angry things toward others. But the things we do actually come back and hurt no one but us.

The negativity comes back even faster when it is directed toward a person who is higher on the spiritual path than the sender. By higher, I don't necessarily mean a Fifth Initiate as opposed to a Third. What I am saying is that anyone on the path of ECK who has a pure heart has the full protection of the Master, which means the full protection of the ECK. This is not to say that there won't be hardships along the way; but when the chips stop flying, the person with the pure heart is going to come out of it better than the other.

Completing Cycles

After I gave a talk at the recent seminar in Hawaii, the ECK was flowing through so strongly that I knew I had to do something with the energy. It's like a light bulb that's supposed to be carrying sixty watts, and I'm pumping a few hundred through it. So when one of the staff said, "I found a video parlor," I just said, "Wonderful." What better place to find a person who needed the flow more than I did at that moment?

96

Our group set off for the video parlor, but the traffic was so heavy that the farther we drove, the more reasons we came up with to turn back. Maybe this wasn't the best time to go play video games, we figured. Finally we decided not to go.

Our plane was to leave a little after midnight, so we packed and went to the airport. When we got there we were told that the flight had been delayed three hours. There was absolutely nothing else to do but go back to the video parlor.

Sometimes life gives you an opportunity—a single window—through which you can have an experience. But when that window appears, you have to step through it. So when the Mahanta comes with that opportunity—whether through Soul Travel, in the dream state, or in contemplation—you have to be willing to go. If the Inner Master says, "Come with me," then just go; don't worry about anything. You will be enriched many times over.

Some people may think it's funny for the Living ECK Master to play video games, but it's not funny, it's necessary. After two hours of playing, I finally felt more like a human being than an overtaxed light bulb.

I couldn't help wondering if the others in our group had noticed that we hadn't completed a cycle that afternoon. But the ECK arranges what is needed. I'm grateful for that.

Co-workers with God

There is always a way to spread the message of ECK, even in video parlors. People do communicate with each other, even if only by way of the electronic scoreboard.

An individual who is very good at Commando went to a video parlor with the goal of topping the current high score. He ended up with 171,000—far above the previous record of 114,000. Despite envious looks from some of the local champs, the ECKist proudly displayed his score on the board next to the name *ECKANKAR*. The next time he achieved the high score on a machine, he listed himself as *Co-worker.*

To become a Co-worker with God is what we are trying to achieve in ECKANKAR. We are not striving to reach a heaven where we sit around and enjoy life everlasting, without personal growth or unfoldment.

Such an existence would be useless for an ECKist. It would be a form of hell to have achieved the highest state you can ever reach and have nowhere left to go. Worse, if everybody else has reached the same heights, then you are all equal. This kind of paradise would probably be hard to take—especially if you got stuck there for an eternity.

One More Step

Heaven in ECK is recognizing that there is always one more step in our quest for consciousness. No matter how far we go, there is always one more step.

This may be a chilling thought for the competitive mind. An ambitious person wants to be at the top in anything he does. When you tell him that there is no top rung on the ladder of God—that there is always one more rung—he might just say, "That doesn't make sense. It's not logical."

And that's entirely the point: The path of ECK is not logical, it's spiritual. Logic is a discipline of the mind; ECK goes beyond the mind.

Besides the mind, we also have the emotions at play as we face the difficult events in our life. We cry and get caught up in an emotional swell, or we strain our mental gears in an attempt to figure out how to solve the problem.

But if we can learn to turn our problems over to Divine Spirit or the Mahanta—which is nothing more than a very high state of consciousness—we can benefit from what I call the Golden-tongued Wisdom. This is an aspect of the ECK-Vidya, the ancient science of prophecy, whereby an individual is able to gain insight into his life on a need-to-know, moment-to-moment basis.

Test Kit

The international airlines cut back on the amount of baggage a passenger may carry on board, so my wife and I take very little with us when we travel. I carry only a single, smaller bag.

At the airport in Sydney, I managed to get my bag through the security check with no problem. Then the official had second thoughts. "Your bag is too big," he said. "If it doesn't fit in the test kit over there, you're going to have to check it."

This was a bother for me because I'd packed all kinds of paperwork to review during the flight. And since tired travelers are not always reasonable or understanding, I stood my ground and gave the airline official a really hard glare. But it had no effect on him. "The test kit is over there," he said, pointing.

My wife and I trudged over to this metal box which is supposed to measure the size of a bag and determine whether it qualifies to be taken on board. I was pretty sure my bag wouldn't fit.

"Put the bag on the seat over here," my wife said. "If you empty the side pocket, it will fit."

"It's a waste of time," I argued. "They aren't going to let me take this bag on board."

"Just empty it," she insisted.

I removed all my books and papers from the side pocket and put them on another chair. She zipped the bag shut, took it back to the test kit, and stuffed it in. "This fits, sir," she said to the official. "Does it pass?"

"It's OK," he said.

As soon as we moved out of his sight, I stuffed my papers into a plastic bag and gave it to another passenger who had no baggage of his own to carry on. Sometimes we have to think outside of the square, in this case, outside of the test kit.

Listening as Soul

When we're tired, we don't always listen; as Soul—the inner Self—we are always being guided by the ECK. The inner direction comes to us intuitively, but if we don't pay attention, we find hardships put in our way.

When the man said, "You can't take this bag on board," all I saw was a several-hour flight with nothing to work on. In my state of weariness, this seemed like a hardship. But it worked out anyway, because my wife was paying attention—and I listened to her. If you can't listen to your spouse, how can you listen to the ECK?

Each of us is Soul, and Soul is a highly creative unit. But some people are more open to the Light of ECK than others. They are more spiritually attuned beings.

Walt Disney was one such individual. He was an artist in a world of moneymakers. While many got involved in cartoons for the sake of profit, Disney did it to make people happy. He was trying to show them something.

Walt Disney's Vision

Next month is the fiftieth anniversary of Walt Disney's *Snow White and the Seven Dwarfs*. The first full-length cartoon feature, *Snow White* marked a turning point in film animation. Up to this point, cartoons were very short, running only a few minutes in length.

Disney saw a trend occurring in the film industry. New trends, whether in government, the film industry, or anywhere else, signify an evolutionary jump. It's usually a push toward making something greater and better than in the past.

This is also true for the individual Soul. We find it easy to believe in ourselves, of course, but not in our neighbor. We believe we are growing greater in the grace of God, but our neighbor is not. How could he be? He's opinionated, bullheaded, argues incessantly with us, and doesn't accept our way of looking at things. It's interesting how much better we know our neighbor than we know ourself.

Disney was faced with the creative challenge of making a cartoon that was ten times longer than usual. He had a good enough understanding of human nature to know he would run into resistance to something new. Yet, he had watched the trend develop in other areas of the film industry. Both Charlie Chaplin and the Keystone Kops had started in very short movies; they were now in longer and longer features. This was a byproduct of the progression into the use of color and sound. These manifestations of the Light and Sound of ECK are all around us, even here.

And so in film there was a growing trend toward longer presentations. But a cartoon? Disney knew his artists would have a reaction when he told them what he had in mind, so he softened them up before the meeting

101

by treating all thirty-five of them to dinner. Back on the sound stage, he laid out his plans.

"We are going to animate a Grimm's fairy-tale, *Snow White and the Seven Dwarfs*," he said, then proceeded to act out all the different characters—Snow White, the wicked queen, the prince, and each of the seven dwarfs.

The creativity of Soul came through this man so strongly that, by the time he finished his presentation, his artists were caught up in the spirit of his vision.

The film took three years to make. While the number of artists and support staff grew to nearly seven hundred, Disney demanded excellence in every drawing. Out of well over two million drawings, 477,000 were selected and ended up in a feature that ran an hour and twenty-three minutes.

A lot of hurdles had to be jumped to reach that point. Disney not only named the dwarfs, he tried to create seven distinct personalities. One particular trait was inspired by an experience he'd had years ago on an overnight outing with a group of men. With all of them crowded into one room, he lay awake all night listening to the noises the others made while they slept. That's when he realized that each man has a unique snore. Thus, each dwarf was given his own unique snore.

States of Soul

In the seven dwarfs we actually see many of our own states of consciousness. There's Bashful—the bashful Soul, off by Itself, the odd man out. Then there's Sleepy, which we often are spiritually, and Sneezy, who shows what can happen when we have a reaction to the world around us.

Other dwarfs were paired, in a way, to illustrate the opposing forces that strive for balance in each of us.

102

Grumpy and Happy, for example. Doc, who thinks he knows everything, and Dopey, who never tries anything. They represent the positive and negative currents that work within us at all times. But there is also a third energy—the spiritual or the neutralizing current—which tries to achieve a balance between the other two.

Walt Disney may not have dug this deeply, but he knew people. In his dwarfs he put many characteristics of the human consciousness. So many, in fact, that the dwarfs are more human than most people in the story.

Striving for Excellence

He was also receptive to the creative ideas of others who saw ways to improve the film. One artist experimented with giving one of the dwarfs a happy little half-jump to get himself in step as they marched off to work. This is where they sing, "Heigh-ho, heigh-ho, it's off to work we go."

As soon as Disney saw it, he said, "That's great." He asked the artists to go back to the very beginning of the series of drawings and put in the little jump wherever the seven dwarfs were marching. It required an enormous amount of work, but Walt Disney was striving for excellence.

Soul strives for excellence more than for perfection. Perfection assumes a state beyond which nothing better can exist. But excellence means being the very best you can at any particular time.

When the film was pretty far along in production, Disney ran out of money. Another half million dollars was needed to finish it. Since he had already borrowed to the hilt from all the sources available to him, somehow he had

103

to prove to the bank that he could repay the additional money. The bank sent one of its directors to the studio, where Disney took him into a viewing room.

A Hatful of Money

If ever the creativity of Soul was working through a human being, it was the time Walt Disney tried to sell an unfinished cartoon to a profit-conscious bank executive. Handicapped by the fact that much of the film hadn't been put together yet, Disney had to improvise. He screened whatever film clips he had available and personally acted out for the banker all the parts that were yet to be completed.

When the presentation was over, the banker got up and walked out of the room without saying a word about the film. Disney was crestfallen. He saw everything he had struggled for going down the drain.

He escorted the banker out to the parking lot. Just as he was about to say good-bye, the man looked at him and said, "That thing is going to make you a hatful of money!" Disney knew he had the loan.

The result was the first of the magical, spiritual, full-length films from the wonderful world of Disney.

Working for Your Goals

Walt Disney's story is an example of the inner creative element coming to the front. Walt Disney had a dream, but he also realized it would take more than wishing to make it come true. To accomplish something in this life, you have to work for it.

Once you learn to sing HU, the holy word of God, you begin to open yourself to the spiritual help needed to accomplish your goals. With each goal you accomplish, you grow stronger in Spirit; you become a fuller spiritual being.

As this happens, you more and more become the Sound and Light of ECK. Your light becomes much greater than before. People come up to you just to be near you. They don't know why, of course, but it's because they can feel the Light and Sound that is coming through you.

Feed My Kangaroos

On the inner planes I met a number of ECKists who worked on a farm. They kept looking up at the cloudy sky, trying diligently to bring in hay from the fields before the rain started. I was sitting on a tractor not far from the field when one of the ECKists spotted me.

"Bring that tractor and hay wagon over here," he called. "We can load it with hay and get it inside before the rain comes." So I drove over to them, and they loaded it.

We pulled up next to a building, and they began throwing bales of hay through a window.

"Hey, wait a minute," I said. "You're throwing hay into my bedroom." I was sharing the room with Peddar Zaskq (Paul Twitchell). "We sleep there, you know."

These ECKists may have looked like farmers, but they sure didn't know how to tie a bale. The strings were not adjusted properly, and the bales fell apart when we tried to pick them up. Hay was strewn all over the floor and the beds.

"We've done this before when it was going to rain," they answered. "There are some animals coming in, and they have to be fed."

"What's up there?" I asked, pointing to an upper window. We climbed a ladder and looked in the second-floor window. There were thousands of stock pens below. Trucks were being backed up the hill to the second floor, and priests in black coats were unloading truckload after truckload of kangaroos.

"How many?" I called to one of the priests.

"Fourteen thousand," he said.

Spiritual Food

The experience meant a lot spiritually. The kangaroos symbolized the springiness of Soul—happy, bouncing, always jumping around. The truckloads represented the many people ready to come to ECK from other religions. Some of the clergy from the other religions realize that certain of their people are ready for ECK, where the spiritual food is plentiful. In their own way, they are helping the people to reach this new level.

ECK initiates must get prepared. Through giving talks and forming Satsang classes, they have to be ready to provide the spiritual food to those who come looking for it.

Can I Come Along?

An ECKist did a spiritual exercise one evening; she began by reading from *Stranger by the River* by Paul Twitchell. She read the chapter called "Practice of the Zikar." *Zikar* means making contact with the Holy Spirit within by chanting a holy word of God, such as HU. Singing the word *HU* is the practice of the Zikar.

This individual chanted HU for a few minutes then contemplated on the chapter she had just read. In it, the ECK Master Rebazar Tarzs is explaining the Zikar to the seeker, Peddar Zaskq. Using a visualization technique, the ECKist imagined herself on the inner planes, requesting permission to walk with them and listen to their conversation.

"Can I come along?" she asked.

"Sure," they said.

Suddenly she was no longer imagining the experience; she was there on the inner planes, walking down a hallway. With her was a man of medium height with a gray-and-white beard. He wore a sport coat over a turtleneck shirt. Later she identified him as the ECK Master Fubbi Quantz.

"Hurry along," he said, motioning her to follow him. He took a set of keys out of his pocket, which she assumed he would use to unlock the door at the end of the hallway. Instead, still holding the keys in his hand, Fubbi Quantz walked right through the wall. This was possible because they were both in the Soul body.

She followed him through the wall and into a room where she saw a bed all covered with pearls. As she gazed at them, she knew they were pearls of wisdom.

A loud noise quickly brought her back from the experience. She found herself at home in bed. Remembering the experience, she felt happy and uplifted.

There is strong imagery at the beginning of each chapter in *Stranger by the River.* My favorite is "The Trembling of a Star." Read a chapter, focus on the imagery, and go into contemplation. Sooner or later you may have an inner experience of your own.

The Spiritual Exercises of ECK are designed to help you into the higher states of consciousness so that you may become a greater spiritual being, and one day a Co-worker with God.

Australian Regional Seminar, Perth, Australia,
Saturday, November 28, 1987

Watching her, it occurred to me that we have to be as hungry for ECK, for the Holy Spirit, as she was for food.

7

Know What You Want

Earlier today my wife and I were coming out of the hotel restaurant. A husband and wife, who appeared to be in their early sixties, were just entering the hotel lobby. He carried their suitcases over to the check-in desk, but she, with a glazed look in her eyes, turned and headed in the direction of the restaurant.

Her husband looked kind of startled. "Hey, where are you going?" he called after her. But she was out of earshot by then, marching straight to a table. She knew exactly what she wanted, and nothing was going to stop her. Watching her, it occurred to me that we have to be as hungry for ECK, the Holy Spirit, as she was for food.

Reach Out for God

Recently I was talking with someone about the joy we find once we learn how to travel in the worlds of God, whether in the dream state, through Soul Travel, or by just being there. It is practically impossible to tell anyone what it's like in those other worlds. It is no exaggeration to say that some of the buildings and rooms are immense in size—twenty or thirty times larger than here—and hold throngs of people.

The most that anyone can do, including the Living ECK Master, is to tell those who want the higher experiences of God about the Spiritual Exercises of ECK. We can encourage them to try these for themselves. All that anyone can do for others, really, is to inspire them to reach out for God themselves.

When I say reach out for God, I mean to reach the state of Godhood that resides within each of us. This is the high state of ECK consciousness, the consciousness of the Holy Spirit.

This is a very difficult thing to do. But once one begins to experience the Light and Sound of ECK, even if it is before coming on the path of ECKANKAR, he or she is a changed person. From then on there is always the hunger, always the longing for that indefinable something which is always out of reach, always out of sight, but never out of mind.

Worlds of Joy

When people come across the path of ECK, they learn that if they make an effort and work with expectation and excitement, they too can reach into the worlds of joy. The worlds of God are worlds of joy and light. The earth, in comparison, is a very dark place.

But the brightness of the other worlds cannot be explained, it can only be experienced. This is why we call ECK the path of experience.

We don't ask others to believe what we tell them about the other worlds and the people who reside there, or that this is the true home of Soul. All we can do is offer to show them how to do a simple spiritual exercise. If they are interested, we tell them to close their eyes and chant HU.

Knowing this is a sacred name for God, we do it with love. Then we show them how to do it.

Showing a person how to chant HU is sometimes the best introduction to ECK that you can give. Then it is up to the individual to reach out and meet the Inner Master, whom we know as the Mahanta.

Talking to God

A young girl had an intense longing to know God. It started just before her sixteenth birthday, when she became very ill. The doctor gave her penicillin, but she suffered an allergic reaction to it.

She awoke during the night to find her hands so swollen that she couldn't get her rings off. They felt too tight. Walking to the bathroom on wobbly legs, she used soap and water to remove the rings.

Back in bed she began to feel frightened. She couldn't swallow, and it was becoming difficult to breathe. She called to her father, usually a very light sleeper, but he didn't answer. Always before, whenever she was sick, all she had to do was call out and her father would come immediately. But this time, even after three more tries, he still didn't come.

Too weak to get out of bed again, she said to herself, "I'll just talk to God." In her own way, she was trying to reach the highest state of help that she could.

She called out to God, and at that moment a light appeared in her room. Unafraid, she began to talk to the light. As a person of the Christian consciousness will often do, she apologized to God for whatever she had done wrong that might have caused her to be sick. She threw in everything she could think of, so this went on for quite a while.

Suddenly the light became even brighter, and she realized that she was out of her body. She was listening to the most beautiful music she had ever heard.

From then on, she had an intense longing to find the meaning of this experience of Light and Sound. She never really understood it until several years later, when she came to ECKANKAR. That led to many more experiences with the Light and Sound and with the Inner Master.

Meeting the Mahanta

Usually, though not always, the Light comes first. Then comes the Sound. When the two parts come together within you, the Mahanta, the Inner Master, appears. This is the high consciousness of God.

Once the Mahanta is established within you, still other changes come about. You may go for weeks or months without seeing the Master or having conscious experiences with the Light and Sound. Yet, eventually you come to the point where you are aware that this God Force is always with you, in one way or another.

You know that It is always working within you—to make your life better, to uplift you in Spirit, and to help you understand why you are having certain problems in your everyday life. When you understand the reasons for the troubles, you can begin to work them out. This, then, will free you to go on to overcome greater problems.

You would probably rather hear that your life at this point will be full of bliss and you will have no more problems. Unfortunately, it's not so. Earth is a classroom. Its purpose is to give Soul the experience It needs to become, first, a Co-worker with the Mahanta, and then a Co-worker with God. This is part of the progression of Soul.

Know What You Want

A man who knew what he wanted showed up at an ECK Center one evening. The ECKist who was there to greet visitors had busied himself arranging the books and posters. While he was in the back room, he suddenly heard a loud noise at the front door. It sounded like someone was banging on it with a sledgehammer. He peered out the window and saw a police car parked on the street. Outside stood a police officer with a very stern look on his face.

When the ECKist opened the door, the first thing the officer did was stick his head in and look around, as though to make sure it was safe. Only then did he enter. The ECKist waited politely to see what he wanted, but the officer didn't say anything.

"Would you like to sit down?" the ECKist asked. The officer sat down without saying a word. After a long silence, he finally spoke: "What is this ECKANKAR about, anyway?"

The ECKist talked with him for two hours. By the time the officer left, he had several ECK books under his arm and was ready to request membership in ECKANKAR.

It was Soul—the police officer—who had come to find out about ECK. The officer was merely following the inner urging of his true Self. Soul knew what It wanted. It had a longing to hear about something for which It did not have any words. It wanted the way home to God, and this is what the police officer found that evening.

The Wind of ECK

The wind of ECK often comes so unexpectedly that we mistake it for something else. After studying the ECK discourses for six months, an individual who lived in Florida still hadn't had a conscious experience with the

Light or Sound. Another ECKist gave him tips on how to chant HU so that he would have more success with his spiritual exercises.

One night he was at home in contemplation, and nothing was happening. Suddenly a high wind began blowing outside the house. The gusts were so strong that he wondered if there was a hurricane warning in effect. But he wasn't alarmed; he just sat there listening to the sound of the wind blowing and blowing.

The next morning he went to check on the elderly woman who lived next door. "I hope the wind didn't scare you last night," he said.

She looked puzzled. "I didn't hear anything," she said. "There was no wind last night."

"No wind?"

"None," she said.

He checked with several other people in the neighborhood. All of them confirmed that there hadn't been any wind the night before. He realized then that he had heard one of the sounds of ECK, which had come to purify and uplift him. These sounds are the kiss of God.

On the Razor's Edge

The most difficult thing to overcome as I present the teachings of ECK is the misinformation people have about God, about the Holy Spirit, and about heaven. Everything I say is weighed and judged according to what the individual has been taught before.

It is not my intention to leave someone without a point of reference; therefore I do not get into strong arguments designed to convince them of this or that. Instead, I present examples, images, and spiritual exercises. These may inspire people to try to reach the inner worlds themselves, where there can be no doubt.

A person hearing about ECK for the first time may feel pretty good about it while he is at the talk. But after he leaves, a reaction sets in. Suddenly he feels exposed, uncovered; as if somehow he has forsaken the safety of his old religion.

This is when doubt begins to tear away at him. He knows the message of the Light and Sound of God sounds true, but at this point he only has someone else's word for it. In a sense, he is on the razor's edge. He is torn between the truth of ECK and whatever truth he feels his present religion offers him.

Inner Strength

The inner struggle then begins as the ECK starts coming into him with pure truth. It brings changes in such a way that he may not know what is happening to him. Personal relationships seem to hit the shoals; his inner life is like a ship at sea in a storm.

Then gradually the ECK—the pure consciousness of truth—begins to create a spiritual foundation within the individual. Things balance out. All of a sudden the Light and Sound begin to come in, bringing him a greater awareness. He comes to realize that all the problems were nothing more than karma he had to work off in order to come into a fuller understanding of life.

The Golden-tongued Wisdom

The Golden-tongued Wisdom is an aspect of the ECK-Vidya, the ancient science of prophecy. In ECK, prophecy has a broader definition than just seeing the future. It also includes having the awareness to perceive the spiritual

115

truth in a situation, or to understand the relationship between yourself and another person in a way that no one else can.

An ECKist from a Christian background decided to write a book about his new understanding of Christianity. It mentioned nothing at all about ECK, yet it was written from the ECK consciousness.

When the ECKist's manuscript was completed, he sought out someone to typeset it for him. Out of the listings he found in the yellow pages, one name kept popping out at him. This is one way the Golden-tongued Wisdom works. It was the Holy Spirit telling him: There is a reason why you should contact this person.

Typesetting a Manuscript

The typesetter was a woman who worked in her home. "This is an interesting title," she said when he presented her with his manuscript. "Sounds different." He explained what was covered in the book so she wouldn't be put off by it.

They discussed a price, but she wasn't quite sure whether or not she wanted to take on the job. "I'll look it over on the weekend and let you know," she said.

When he came back the following week, she said she'd gone through the manuscript, reading the Bible to double-check some of the references. She had found the material very intriguing. Though raised a Catholic, she had given it up a few years before because it hadn't offered the answers she was looking for.

"At the same time," she said, "I was half-watching the television. There was a program on about a religion I

116

wasn't familiar with, and I couldn't figure out what they were talking about."

All of a sudden, a single phrase jumped out at her. The words were simply this: Spirit of the unwritten truth.

This was a form of the Golden-tongued Wisdom. The experience came because she was reading about ECK—though the writer had put it in veiled terms—and was very receptive to It.

"Then I heard the strangest sound," she said.

"What kind of a sound?" he asked.

"It sounded like the buzzing of bees," she answered. In ECK we know this is how the Sound occurs on the Etheric Plane, the level that corresponds with the high part of the mind, the unconscious mind. It comes just before the Soul Plane, so at that point she was actually very high in consciousness to be able to hear that Sound.

The ECKist knew that he would be seeing more of her in the future. As she worked on the book, she would have the opportunity to learn more about ECK. After that, she could go on to learn as much as she wanted to know.

Writers in ECK

In their own way, the ECK writers will do much to introduce people to the teachings of ECK. They will find ways, whether quietly or openly, to point out how much better life can be when viewed with understanding and knowledge.

This can help a person gain insight into why life is dealing him a certain hand. He can begin to see why he is in certain situations. If the individual gets into ECK, he will eventually have his own glimpses into the Causal Plane, where the karmic seeds which now affect his outer life were created.

117

Soul Knows

Soul knows what It wants even if the human consciousness does not. This is one of the ways the ECK reaches the human consciousness. Soul has often met the Mahanta, the Inner Master, months or even years before the individual comes in contact with the teachings of ECK.

From the time this first meeting occurs on the inner planes, there is an intense longing that cannot be explained. But in ECK we know that God is love, and this longing is a desire for the love of God. With the love of God comes a joy and happiness that can only be known through personal experience.

Soul as a Co-worker

Another individual had an experience with the Sound during a crucial time in her life many years before she'd heard of ECK. The sound of a flute woke her up from a deep sleep in the middle of the night.

Her first groggy impression was that there was a flute player in the house. She even got up to check all the rooms in her home. The next time it happened, she began to wonder where this sound of the flute came from. It was beautiful; always uplifting and comforting.

After she came into ECKANKAR, she began to see the Light. With It came the Inner Master. Some time later she began to work on the inner planes, helping the spiritual hierarchy escort people across who were ready to leave this life but didn't know about ECK.

One time she awoke in one of the spiritual worlds to find herself in a large department store. She was trying on hats. This experience represented her ability to see herself in a number of different ways. It meant she was getting closer to seeing life from a 360-degree viewpoint.

Escort to the Other Side

She went out in the hallway to wait for an older woman who was walking toward her. "Are you ready?" the ECKist said kindly. "Yes," the woman answered, but she didn't sound too sure. The ECKist knew that somewhere on earth this woman was leaving the physical body, and that she was a little bit uncomfortable and uncertain about what was to come.

Together they walked to the door at the end of the hallway. The ECKist reached into her purse and took out a key. She unlocked the door and pushed it open to reveal a long staircase that went up to the sky.

The ECKist didn't mention anything about ECK; she realized the woman didn't have the awareness to deal with this knowledge. But as a Co-worker with the Mahanta, she escorted the woman to the end of the stairway, where she was greeted by those who would look after her on the other side.

A person who translates, or dies, before coming into ECK is often greeted by departed relatives. After you come into ECK, it is the Mahanta who meets you, sometimes accompanied by your friends and relatives. The higher worlds are so bright and the state of consciousness so delightful that, once you get there, you don't give another thought to the heavy human body left behind in this dark, old world.

As we go along in ECK, we become more and more a Co-worker with the Mahanta. This is a high state of spiritual consciousness. There are many ways to be a co-worker, and the following story illustrates one more.

An Alternate Route

Late one night, an ECK initiate was driving home from her brother's wedding reception. She knew the way very well, but she felt a strong nudge from the Inner Master to take an alternate route. She hesitated, of course, because it didn't make any sense. But the inner urge was so strong that she made a sharp turn onto the unfamiliar road.

All of a sudden she smelled smoke. A little farther along, she drove right into a thick wall of smoke. To the left she saw a garage on fire. The garage was attached to a house.

Since it was late at night, the ECKist was pretty sure that the people inside were sound asleep. She jumped out of the car and pounded on the front door to wake them up. They immediately called the fire department. Next to the garage was a garden hose, which she used to spray water on the flames until the fire truck arrived.

Being of Service to Life

Later, as the ECKist drove home, she realized that she had been there to save the family's lives simply because the Master had urged her to turn down that road. Because she had listened, she was able to serve as a co-worker, to save these people from unnecessary grief. It was karma they did not need to go through.

At the same time, a link was formed between the ECKist and the people in the house. It was an outer link at this point, but because of it, she had a feeling the Inner Master would soon appear to one of the members of the family.

There is nothing to compare with the feeling of being of service to life. Once we get into the higher states of awareness, a dramatic change takes place: Never again are we satisfied to serve only ourselves. In one way or another, we must serve all life.

Country Music Serenade

One summer, an ECKist was on a flight to an ECKANKAR seminar when she began to feel a little queasy. Ordinarily she didn't get motion sickness, so she attributed it to the bumpy ride and being seated in the smoking section near the back of the plane. A concerned stewardess was able to move her to a seat closer to the front.

Still, the woman didn't feel too comfortable. To try to relax and settle her stomach, she shut her eyes and began to chant HU. She was so busy feeling sick that she was caught completely off guard when the Mahanta appeared in her inner vision—wearing a ten-gallon hat and fringed buckskin jacket, with a guitar strapped over his shoulder. As if that wasn't enough of a surprise, he began to strum the guitar and sing the words to an old Hank Williams song.

"Why can't I free your doubtful mind and melt your cold, cold heart?" the Master sang. And the woman realized her physical reactions were not from the plane ride at all. Soul was undergoing a purification before she got to the seminar. Certain attachments and attitudes were causing her doubt and holding her back. The Master was trying to get her to open her heart, to receive the pure teachings of ECK with the attitude of the Golden Heart.

The experience made her giggle out loud, but she quickly settled down when the woman sitting next to her gave her a funny look.

After the ECKist returned home from the seminar, she

went to a meeting at the ECK Center. One of the other initiates was talking to the group about the elusive nature of the Sound of God. Attempting to explain it in terms they could understand, he said, "The Sound of ECK is like classical music. People can try to hum portions of it, but they can never quite capture the beauty and harmony of the entire melody." Then he added, "That doesn't apply to something like country music, of course."

The woman who'd had the experience on the plane couldn't help laughing. "I'd like to tell you a story about that," she said. The initiate who was so sure that classical music was the only form of musical exaltation on earth was about to have a lesson.

The woman told the group how the Master had come to her in the guise of a country singer and sung the Hank Williams song. Everybody had a good laugh about it, because they got the point: Even country music has its place. She said, "I learned that the ECK will reach you in whatever way It can, in whatever way you are open to It. Whether it's through classical music, country music, or anything else, in one way or another the Light and Sound will reach you."

Her experience of seeing and hearing the Inner Master was the Light and Sound combined. The Light formed into the outer appearance of the Master, and the Sound was heard as his song.

Spirit of the Unwritten Truth

ECK is the Spirit of the Unwritten Truth. It is the music of God, the music of the spheres which the ancients spoke about. It is the reality many are seeking to find. Those in ECK who work with the spiritual exercises have found this Sound and Light of God.

Thank you for coming to the seminar. If I seem to end a talk rather abruptly, it's because suddenly I can see that the consciousness in the room is full. I keep going until it fills up, then anything else is like pouring more water into a full glass.

I hope this weekend has brought you spiritual enlightenment and realization. Even if you don't remember a word that was spoken here, you can still carry away with you the love of God.

You will probably notice that the people at home are more drawn to you than usual for a while. The ECK Current, which is the Holy Spirit, generally stays with you very strongly for about a week. It then moves quietly into the background of your life as you begin to unfold into a greater understanding of the Light and Sound of God.

Australian Regional Seminar, Perth, Australia,
Sunday, November 29, 1987

The farther you move toward the mountain of God, the more aware you become of the ECK, the Wind from Heaven.

8

The Wind from the Mountain

The Wind from the Mountain is the ECK. It is that which is spoken of in the movie *Star Wars* as the Force. The ECK is the Life Force we know and respect as the source of our being. It is the fountain of love.

Wind of Change

As the wind comes down from the mountain of God, it brings changes into our lives. We may accept these changes as part of the conditions of life, the spirit of life, or we may resist them. To accept the changes is to accept a greater amount of happiness; to resist is to bring unhappiness to ourselves.

I try to pass along information about the spiritual worlds to people who want to know about heaven in this lifetime. The ECK dream discourses were written so that those who wish to learn more about the worlds invisible to the human eye may have the opportunity to do so. There is awareness on all planes, and your experiences may run from the physical, visible world to the unseen worlds.

Today's Heaven

As you become aware of the inner planes, especially the Astral Plane, you find that some heavens are similar to what you see out here. It is unlikely that you will see cities made of precious stones, as reported in some of the older scriptures. Such inner experiences were interpreted in terms of what was of value to that older culture. By the same token, your world of dreams will in some way reflect heaven as it is today.

We have to recognize that heaven is not a static place. Spiritual evolution continues in all the lower worlds. The sort of heaven that people found two thousand years ago is not necessarily the destination of those who explore the inner worlds today.

A religion that becomes fixed in a time period thousands of years ago refuses to acknowledge that life is change. Our technology has changed so drastically in two thousand years only because the outer experience is a reflection of what is happening on the inner planes. And note that I said, what *is* happening. The inner worlds—those above the physical but below the Soul Plane—are undergoing changes too. Beyond the Soul Plane there is no change in terms of time and space.

While Carrying Groceries

I was walking along the street in the other worlds when I saw an elderly man, probably pushing eighty, carrying a heavy bag of groceries. He was staggering under the load, and I assumed it was because he no longer had the strength of his youth. Age has caught up with that poor old gentleman, I thought.

A couple of young boys ran past and accidentally

126

bumped into him. The old man tottered for a moment, as if he were going to tip over and fall down.

I went up to him and said, "I can carry that bag for you, if you'd like." I knew he lived just half a block away. Looking like he was really happy to get rid of it, he quickly lofted the thing right into my arms. It was so heavy that it knocked me over backward, and I landed flat on my back on the sidewalk.

After I fell down clutching the bag, which now felt like it was loaded with lead bricks, the old man held out his hand. "Can I help you up?" he offered.

That was too much. "I think I can do it myself," I said. Rocking back and forth, I managed to hoist myself up, still holding onto his bag. I was very careful not to damage anything in it. We continued down the street, and I couldn't help noticing that he walked just as steadily as I had before I took on his load.

He shared a house with several other men in a poor section of town. Inside he led me to his private living area, and I carried the bag in and set it on a counter. He thanked me for the help, and I left.

Pointing a Finger at Others

I had formed the opinion that the old man's problem was his failing strength. I was so sure of my assessment that when I offered my help, it was from the wrong perspective. The man didn't care that I had mistaken his problem, of course; he was just glad to have someone else carry the heavy load.

The experience reminded me of how often we presume to judge what goes on in other people's lives. The reason for their problems seems so obvious to us that we just know if they would do this and that, everything would be fine. We decide in our own mind that their troubles are caused by some kind of a failing, and we are quick to identify it as a spiritual weakness. "This person's problems are caused by his lack of self-discipline," we proclaim. But I suspect if we looked at ourselves a little more carefully, we would find that we are the ones having a difficult time with self-discipline.

The Mirror Principle

When you point a finger at another, you are really pointing it at yourself. This is the mirror principle that works in the spiritual life.

It is when we arrogantly make wrong assessments of what other people have wrong with them that the wind comes down from the mountain. The ECK sweeps into our life and blows away the leaves which are no longer appropriate for the season. Without knowing why, our life has become as difficult as that of the person we were pointing a finger at.

I have seen this happen so often: When someone points the finger of criticism at another, it isn't too long before he goes through the very same problem that he mislabeled when it happened to the other person. Why? Because the Wind from the Mountain, which is the ECK, or Holy Spirit, has come down and the spiritual currents are making a change. The purpose is to bring truth into the life of the observer. It occurs in his own life because he—and each of us—is the living truth.

What the Initiates Need

The material that I accumulate for these seminar talks is not always what I would like to present. It is what is supposed to be given. When the ECK says, "This is information the ECK initiates need to know," I put it in a file folder and don't look at it again until I get to the seminar. I use the principle of trusting the ECK.

My preparation for a talk takes place over a period of months. I look for topics that fit the spiritual needs of the times. I try to find examples that demonstrate spiritual principles. I want to give you a clearer understanding of the psychology of Spirit. In some way, then, you can get an idea of how the ECK and the laws of life operate.

Draw Back the Curtain

Imagine a curtain hanging in front of an individual who is looking for truth. He is able to see well enough on this side of the curtain. This is where he finds only the most apparent, shallow, superficial truths which occur in one's everyday life.

Through the Spiritual Exercises of ECK, he begins to draw back the curtain. This allows him to see how the greater part of life operates on the other side.

This curtain is not pulled back in one fell swoop. The individual does not get a great gust of instant Self-Realization (which comes at the Soul Plane) or God-Realization (which comes at one of the higher planes). Rather, it's as if the curtain that hides the true laws and mysteries of life is actually made up of many different layers of cloth.

Degrees of Realization

As each layer of the curtain is pulled back, the individual is given another degree of realization. This is the point where he can say, "Ah! The things I have learned lately, through my own experiences, have come together. Now I understand a little bit more about the workings of life."

The experiences continue—some difficult, some happy and uplifting—until at some point he is able to go up to the curtain and draw back another layer of cloth. This time he sees even more. Each layer he pulls out of the way allows him a fuller view of life as it is being manifested from the other planes of God down into this world.

As the dreamer, you are learning to walk through this curtain that separates the physical plane from the other worlds. As you enter the other worlds through one of the techniques of higher consciousness—dream travel, Soul Travel, direct perception or beingness—you are able to see life in its greater format. You develop an understanding of spiritual realities which are not shared by those outside of ECK. They're not always shared by fellow ECKists, either.

Swings of Life

Sometimes we tend to group all ECKists together under a blanket statement. We might say, "ECKists are more spiritually evolved than those who are not in ECK." That may be true in some cases, but not necessarily in all. Each of you is Soul and is at a different level of understanding. And each of you operates differently in regard to the laws of life.

At times you are higher. Then, as the swings of life go, for a while you operate at a lower level. But then you go up again. It is almost like driving along a road through the foothills toward the mountain: sometimes you go up, sometimes down.

But despite the ups and downs of your journey, the farther you drive, the higher you actually go. The farther you go toward the mountain of God, the more aware you become of the ECK, the Wind from Heaven.

Finding What Works

In one of the African countries, the ECK leaders require all initiates to be well versed in the ECK books, such as *The Shariyat-Ki-Sugmad,* which is the ECK bible. They must know the principles of ECK inside-out and every other way you can think of. If an initiate is at an ECK activity and one of the leaders walks up to him and says, "Would you give a ten-minute talk at 10:15 a.m.?" he is expected to give the talk—cold—without any real preparation on the topic given to him.

I once asked some of the ECK leaders from another African country, "Do you expect the same from the ECKists as these Higher Initiates do?" They just smiled gently and said, "No, we do not." The people in that particular country, which was one of the French colonies, are a little more mellow and seem to take life a bit more easy.

It must be tough to come to a seminar expecting to relax and enjoy the program, then have someone tap you on the shoulder and say, "Hello. You're a speaker." But the method works in that area. I don't discourage it. Many high government officials and people at all levels of life are finding the truth of ECK. The initiates are having a great amount of success in spreading the message of ECK.

Each of the ECKists feels ready at any time to speak with authority about the truth of ECK because the teachings play such a large role in their everyday life. It's a hard life, fraught with dangers and day-to-day hardships that are difficult to imagine in Western society. And yet, their trust in ECK is strong. They have many experiences with the Light and Sound of ECK and take them as natural occurrences.

Having Real Spiritual Experiences

When we talk of the Light and Sound of the Holy Spirit, we are not just speaking figuratively, as is often done by those in the orthodox religions. Sometimes they will say, "I feel that God is with me; it is a great experience." Feeling is a part of the spiritual experience, of course. But there is a greater experience—that of actually seeing the Light or hearing the Sound of God.

The Light is seen in any number of colors—blue, yellow, white, or any of the pastel shades. The Sound is the Voice of God, or the ECK. It can be heard as many sounds, even a musical instrument.

Your Spiritual Personality

Those who are familiar with the ways of ECK know that It does not always speak to us in a lofty manner. It often brings us insights through something more down to earth, like a pet. Because of this, we may have a harder time figuring out the spiritual lesson behind the experience.

In your everyday life, if there is an incident that is out of the ordinary, that upsets you greatly, disturbs you, or makes you unusually happy, you can be sure that behind the experience is a lesson the Mahanta is trying to bring across to you. The Mahanta is trying to give you some revelation about yourself; otherwise that experience would not have happened to you.

When something like this occurs, try to see beyond the curtain that hides the meaning of what is going on. The Master is trying to bring you a truth, to give you a little bit more knowledge of your spiritual personality. He's trying to show you who and what you are.

Revelation

The reason this curtain has a number of different layers is simple: If it were torn away all at once, the revelation would be too much. Such a revelation is an uncontrolled spiritual experience. It could throw the truth-seeker into a state of madness and imbalance. It could cause more damage than enlightenment.

Sometimes an individual is misled into putting his hand on the curtain that separates this world from the mysteries of the other worlds and pulling it back all at once. We must remember that revelation comes through seeing the Light of God. When the curtain is pulled back all at once, the Light comes full force. It comes too brightly, too suddenly, too soon. And that can cause the individual to become imbalanced.

One is rarely told this by the teachers of the orthodox religions. They don't know about it. When they speak of seeing the Light of God, they mean it figuratively, in the sense that somehow you will become a better person. They do not recognize that when truth comes, there is an actual, visible Light. It acts as the heating element in the crucible in which Soul is tempered.

In other words, the word of God can also be the fire that purifies Soul. And because this simple truth is not generally understood by the orthodox teachers, it may be just as well that they do not teach it. Not knowing the mechanical elements of the spiritual laws, they cannot give guidance on how to avoid getting too much Light, or how to regulate the Sound that comes to a person.

The Little Orange Cat

One way in which the ECK can bring us truth, or a better realization of ourselves, is through a pet. An ECKist

133

became the owner of a little orange cat that had belonged to a friend of hers. Two days before the cat arrived, the couch she sent out for reupholstering six months earlier was delivered. "Great," her husband said. "Just in time for the cat."

To make the cat comfortable, the woman bought it a deluxe kitty-litter box, which she put on the back porch. Her friend had assured her, "This cat is housebroken and can contain herself all day. You don't have to worry about her while you're at work. Just let her go out on the back porch before you leave in the morning, and she'll be fine until you get home."

So the little orange cat practically came with a guarantee. You know how that goes. It was every bit as good as the guarantees you get with used cars.

One night the woman came home from work to find the cat chewing on some of her aloe-vera plants. It's probably trying to get rid of hair balls, she figured. Naturally she scolded it, thinking that would do the trick. Then, a night or two later, she found the cat had pulled a whole plant right out of the pot and left it lying on the window seat by the bay window. This time the leaves weren't touched at all.

The ECKist was really upset to come home from a hard day's work and find such a mess. All she wanted to do was cuddle her little orange cat, but she felt obligated to scold it first. Then she picked it up and loved and petted it.

While the woman was cleaning up the dirt around the window, she noticed that the shutters were partially opened. So not only did the cat pull the plant out by its roots and leave it lying on the window seat, it apparently had tried to open the shutters. She couldn't figure out what was going on.

She went to the kitchen to get the cleaning materials to finish the job. An artist with very sensitive perceptions,

134

she noticed a strange smell. She wondered if the butter icing on the cake she had left out during the day had gone bad.

But that didn't seem to be causing the odor. She looked all around the kitchen, and as she walked past the sink, she suddenly did a double take. "No!" she shrieked. She could not believe what she saw in there.

Wait a minute, she thought. Could her husband have bought this plastic thing and put it in the sink as a joke? No—it was for real.

Like a good detective, she began to piece together the events. The cat must have had to relieve itself during the day. Since the woman had locked the back door that morning, the cat had had no way to get outside to the litter box. Because she had left the cat in a position where it couldn't win, it had tried to improvise.

First it pulled the plant out of the pot, looking for dirt. But when it saw what was there, it had to conclude, This is not enough.

Seeing light coming in through the shutters, the cat probably said to itself, "I must get outside." It then opened the shutters trying to get out through the window. Failing that, it did the next best thing—it ran into the kitchen and jumped into the sink, where the ECKist found a surprise waiting for her when she got home from work. When she realized how neat the cat had tried to be, she had to laugh. The cleanup took hardly any time at all.

Summarizing what she had learned, she said, "Obviously I put someone I love in a very bad position. The cat has basic needs like everyone else. I was unreasonable to assume that the call of nature would follow the same pattern every day."

Eventually she realized that the Mahanta, this high state of consciousness, had given her a lesson about life in general. What she had learned about the cat also applied to people, at home and at work: If you box someone into a position where they can't win for losing, you have to expect that they are going to find some way out of it.

Advice and Protection

Cats and dogs are smart; they usually understand what you tell them. If they don't do what you say, it's usually because they feel there is some greater reason to disobey your command, and they'll just have to take the consequences.

More often than not, though, I suspect they simply have a different opinion than ours—especially cats. A dog is more likely to do what we say, which is why it's called man's best friend. It knows how to make us feel important, so we can say, "This dog does whatever we want it to. Isn't it smart?"

Dogs are smart enough to flatter their humans shamelessly, because they learn that this is how they can make a good home for themselves. A cat, on the other hand, isn't so mindful of the laws of diplomacy. It isn't concerned with getting along with its betters, because it thinks it *is* the better. If you tell a cat not to sit on a certain chair, it will sit there just because you said not to. No special reason; just principle.

One day the same woman was outside trying to get her car started. It was a cold morning. She was late for work and still had to clean the snow off the windshield. Finally she got the car running and the snow cleared off the window. As she got ready to drive off, something made her glance back at the house. Oh, no! There was the orange cat, sitting among the plants in the bay window, looking out at her. It was doing just what she had told it not to do.

"Shoo!" she yelled, waving her arms—as if that's going to scare a cat away. For a minute, though, it jumped down out of sight, and she thought it took the hint. "Thank God!" she said.

She opened the car door, ready to jump inside—and there was the cat again, peering out the window at her. "Why does this have to happen on a morning when I'm running so late?" she said. But she felt she had no choice. She would have to go back inside and scold the cat.

She stomped up the driveway to the house and put her hand on the doorknob. To her surprise, the door swung open. In her haste to leave, she hadn't pulled it shut firmly enough for the lock to catch. Anyone could have breezed right in and stolen her property.

All of a sudden she realized that the cat was simply trying to tell her, "Mommy, you didn't lock the door!"

The woman felt so badly then. She had assumed that the cat was stubbornly asserting its feline will, when it was only trying to give her a signal about the unlocked door. The Mahanta had worked through the cat, who understood in its own way. It had let her know that something was wrong. The woman did her part too, when she followed the nudge to glance back at the house.

This is an example of the simple little things that occur every day. They don't happen only in the life of an ECKist, but in ECK we do try to be more aware of the seemingly unrelated incidents that appear to be coincidental. Most people, if they made any connection at all, would say, "Oh, isn't it cute that the kitty told me the door wasn't locked? How clever!"

They don't realize that the Wind from the Mountain, the ECK, works through all living beings in some manner. It works through you, your spouse, your children, your neighbors, strangers, and even through your pets. Sometimes the ECKists forget this too.

The Pink Cadillac

Arahatas are the teachers in ECK. At an Arahata training there were thirty-six students and three facilitators experimenting with spiritual exercises. One of the facilitators said, "We're going to divide into four groups of nine people each. We would like each group to come up with its own spiritual exercise."

What they were trying to do was have an experience with the Light and Sound or with the Mahanta. The Mahanta is the Light and Sound of God coming together in a single matrix, which we call the Inner Master. It is often seen as the physical form of myself, which operates on the inner planes as Wah Z, the spiritual name of the Inner Master.

When three of the groups came up with the same exercise, they decided to try it as a class. The spiritual exercise was to chant HU, a holy name for God which is unknown to most of the religions. It is Soul's love song to God, sung as HU-U-U-U-U.

They were to close their eyes and chant HU five times. Using the imagination, they were to let each HU take them to an ever-higher plane. The first HU would take them to the Astral Plane, the second to the Causal Plane, the third to the Mental Plane, the fourth to the Etheric Plane, and the fifth to the Soul Plane. This was to be followed by a period of contemplation. The purpose of the journey was to share a gift with the Mahanta on the Soul Plane.

After the spiritual exercise was over, one of the facilitators volunteered to share his unusual experience. As everyone chanted HU five times, he found himself in the inner worlds, looking at a huge pink Cadillac with shiny gold doodads all over it. "What an ugly car!" he said.

"Get in the car," a voice said to him. "You are to drive that car."

The ECKist was very miffed about this. He didn't go in for showy things, and he hoped no one would see him driving this old pink Cadillac with gold trim through the inner worlds.

When he came to the Mental Plane, the voice said, "Get out of the car. You cannot take it into the Soul Plane."

The car was actually a symbol of the ECKist's inner body. It was still big, clumsy, and overpainted, with too many frills. He hadn't yet refined himself down to an economy-car size, with a nice, eye-pleasing color.

Finally he came to the Soul Plane, where he saw a small Temple of Golden Wisdom. Inside he found the other initiates in the class already gathered there. Just then Wah Z, the Inner Master, came in the door, laughing so hard that he was actually holding his sides. He couldn't even talk.

The facilitator said his experience abruptly ended at this point. Appreciative chuckles came from the group, but one person was laughing harder than all the others. When he got control of himself, he said, "Now I would like to tell you what happened in my inner experience."

He too went up through the inner planes and was one of the initiates waiting in the Wisdom Temple on the Soul Plane when the facilitator arrived, looking very upset. "I saw the whole incident," he said, and went on to tell the rest of the story.

"We were all watching Wah Z, wondering why he was laughing so hard. When he was finally able to talk, he told

139

us, 'You know, I just saw the funniest thing. An ECK initiate came to visit me, and he was driving this awful pink Cadillac.'"

As the facilitator watched the rest of the group's enjoyment of the other initiate's report, he realized that they had fulfilled the purpose of their inner journey. They had shared a gift with the Master, and it was the gift of laughter.

How to Recover When Things Go Wrong

Sometimes when I'm telling a story, even when I have the notes in front of me, I go totally blank. There's nothing worse than getting to the end and forgetting the punch line. When that happens, the joke's on me. But I do the best I can. Somehow I come out of it in one piece.

The Wind from the Mountain, the ECK, occasionally does this to all of us. Just when we think we know exactly what's coming next, the principle is changed. A change is blowing into our life, and all of a sudden everything is different.

We may learn something when things go as expected. But I think we learn a more important lesson in how we recover when things go wrong.

At some point we learn to be gracious enough to accept responsibility for what goes wrong in our life. We know that we did the best we could at that time. And when we can allow others this same charity as we allow ourselves, then we have come a long way on the spiritual path.

ECK Springtime Seminar, Anaheim, California,
Friday, April 1, 1988

The doctor may not have realized it, but as he spoke to the ox, he was sending it love. If we can learn to do all things with love, we have come a long way on our journey home.

9

The Journey Home

"The Journey Home" refers to the experiences that the individual goes through as he tries to reach the highest point of spiritual realization that he can attain. This is Soul's journey home.

Green Apples

An ECKist told me a story about his Second Initiation in ECK, which was given at a seminar many years ago. The initiator was Paul Twitchell.

In preparation for the event, the ECKist went out and bought a bag of green apples. Then he carefully selected the best of the batch to give to Paul at the initiation.

They met at the appointed time, and when the initiation was over, he presented Paul with three fine-looking apples. Paul accepted them graciously, picked one up, and took a bite. Then he proceeded to eat the whole thing. The initiate was very happy that the Master had enjoyed his gift so thoroughly.

Later, during one of his talks, Paul remarked, "While I appreciate the material gifts that you bring me, I would rather have a gift of the heart—the gift of love." The initiate didn't think about it too much at the time, but later he began to wonder if perhaps Paul hadn't liked his gift. Maybe I shouldn't have brought him a gift at all, he thought.

Just before he left for home, the initiate finally reached for one of the green apples from the same batch. It only took one bite for him to realize that it was the sourest thing he had ever tasted.

Paul must have noticed it too, but he had never let on. Could this be what prompted him to say that he would prefer the gift of love over anything material? the initiate wondered. He worried about that for quite a while.

Spiritual Grace

The point that Paul made, through his own example, was this: More important than the things that seem to go wrong in your life is how graciously you are able to respond to them. Are you able to pick yourself up and make the best of a bad situation? Soul, on Its journey home, is learning how to be gracious in a spiritual way.

Once, Paul and his wife, Gail, arrived at a train station within minutes of their departure time. Rushing out to the gate, they found a huge crowd of passengers ahead of them, all waiting to board the train. If everyone ran to the train as soon as the gate opened, there might not be any seats left by the time he and Gail boarded.

But Paul trusted the ECK, which is the Holy Spirit, and just stood there as a pure channel. Rather than fighting his way to the train, he was willing to take any seat he could get, or even stand if he had to.

Suddenly a voice came over the PA system, announcing that the gate number for that departure had been changed. The new gate just happened to be right where he and Gail were standing. Just as the crowd turned and made a mad dash in their direction, the gate opened, and Paul and Gail ended up with choice seats.

Paying Attention

Occurrences like this are common in the life of an ECKist. But the ECKist must be aware enough to observe what is happening to him spiritually. Many people are not.

They have no idea that the ECK is guiding them in a certain direction for their own good. They don't see that these little miracles happen in their lives every day. And not knowing, they complain endlessly about their troubles and the injustices heaped upon them by the shovelful.

"If only the Master would show me exactly how God is showering His grace on me," they say, "then I could be great on the path of ECK." Yet all too often the individual unconsciously shuts his ears to the voice of the ECK, which is the word of God. He is unable to hear the Master's direction.

Temporary Stall

A person might say to me, "If I ever stray on my journey home, please just tell me to my face. Say, 'You haven't been doing so well lately. You're making a mess of your spiritual life, and you aren't doing too well for those around you either.'"

But incredibly enough, a person who is straying on his journey home to God cannot see the direction the Mahanta is trying to give him. Everybody else can see what's happening. Everybody else can tell, for instance, when he is not allowing others the freedom to grow. It remains a secret only to the individual who, at the moment, is sliding backward on the path to God.

Often it is only a temporary backward movement as the person consolidates his spiritual life. When you move forward too fast, you're really packing it in. Sometimes the meaning of what you've gained needs time to settle in.

It's almost as if the individual is unconsciously making time for the experiences to enter his consciousness. Only after this occurs will the experiences actually do him any good.

So when someone wanders off on his journey home, generally I am not able to tell him face-to-face, "You used to be able to follow the path of Light and Sound, but lately you haven't been doing so well." That could be destructive. During the period when the person does not have the awareness to know that he is wobbling on the path, he probably also does not have the ability to catch himself. Therefore, it would be pointless to try to give guidance on the outer by saying, "If you will do this or that, then you will be able to make your life go right." It doesn't work like that.

Unless the individual has an open, loving heart that enables him to accept the inner direction from the Master, the guidance falls on deaf ears. He simply is not able to understand. And so the Master can only stand back and let him have his experience.

The individual's life becomes more difficult, and at some point he comes to realize that he cannot move forward until he understands why he is having such troubles. To do this, he is forced to look back at his most recent experiences and reevaluate what has happened to him. This is when he begins to see how he has shut out the Light and Sound of God.

Dependence upon the ECK

Often this occurs because the individual's life went so smoothly for a while that he lost his humble state of being. There is nothing wrong with the good and happy life, but it can lead to a state of euphoria. Before he knows it, the individual is taking personal credit for everything that goes right. He begins to depend less and less upon the ECK, Divine Spirit.

It's a funny cycle: As one's dependence upon the ECK decreases, he drifts farther from the path. And that's when things begin to go wrong.

Many Paths Home to God

A Catholic priest recently got to see "The Journey Home" video presentation. It was shown to him by a parishioner who had seen the film and wanted the priest's opinion of it.

After the two men watched it together, the parishioner said, "Well, what do you think about ECKANKAR?" The priest said, "There is nothing harmful about these people."

He was open to the fact that there are many paths home to God. We in ECK are following our own expression, our own best way home to God. Our way is not the same as the Catholic way, but there is room for every religious teaching that allows others the freedom to believe as they will.

Knowledge of the Blue Light

An individual who was not a member of ECKANKAR had been seeing things in his inner vision for some time. The images came in the dream state or when he was lying down in a relaxed, half-awake state. They were accompanied by an odd musical sound.

147

Since it had never happened before, it bothered him a great deal. Finally he decided to go for professional counseling.

On his first visit he told the psychiatrist, "When my eyes are closed, I sometimes hear things. I also see a blue light and different people. I get the feeling they're spiritual masters of some kind." He hoped the psychiatrist could help him resolve this problem. But he couldn't.

The man was friendly with an ECK couple, and shortly after he left the psychiatrist, he called them and asked if he could come over. From some of the things he said on the phone, the couple had a feeling that he might be ready to hear about ECKANKAR. At this point, he had no idea that his friends had any knowledge of what the blue light might be.

The couple happened to have a copy of "The Journey Home" video. They invited their friend to watch it with them. At the first mention of the blue light, he quickly said, "That's what I've been seeing! I've seen that blue light!"

"And after you saw the blue light, did you hear any sounds?" one of the ECKists asked. "Like a flute playing?"

"Yes, I did," he said, surprised. "How did you know?"

The film now had a special meaning for him, and he kept his eyes glued to the TV until it was over. It gave him great comfort to learn that others were having the same experiences.

No Longer a Mystery

The two elements of Sound and Light, in any of their many different forms, are emanations of the Voice of God. "The Journey Home" will be very valuable to many people, even those in orthodox religions. Many are having experiences with the Light and Sound but have no one to explain what they mean.

The experience of seeing these manifestations of God's word, which we call the ECK, or Divine Spirit, usually fills them with joy and wonder while they are in that higher state of consciousness. When the experience is over, they try to relate it to others. But nobody knows what they're talking about. Without an explanation for what happened, they start to wonder if there may be something wrong with them.

This video will be a small step in bringing some enlightenment to those who want to learn more about the spiritual realities which ECKists take for granted. It's wonderful to have the experience, but even better to know what it means.

To ECKists, understanding spiritual principles such as karma becomes matter-of-fact knowledge. We stop seeing it as a mystery. It is a natural part of Soul's journey home.

Some ECKists are better at recognizing other people's karma than their own. When someone else has a problem, they'll say, "That's your karma." When something goes wrong in their own life, they say, "Someone is sending me a psychic attack." But since it's our own world, I guess we can make of it what we choose.

Transfer of Karma

An example of karma was given in a book entitled *O Come Ye Back to Ireland,* written by a young couple of Irish descent. Tired of the hassles of living in New York City, they left their urban careers behind to return to their ancestral Ireland.

The couple moved into a cottage in a village on the western coast of Ireland and started getting to know their new community. The book is their account of the clash that takes place when a New-York-City consciousness meets that of rural Ireland. It goes on to tell how each side learned to accommodate the other and came to understand each other's point of view. The result was strong friendships formed in a very short time between the outsiders and the lifelong residents.

One day the couple were invited to a small gathering. A local storyteller was relating some of the tales that had become part of neighborhood lore.

One of the stories was about a farmer who was having bad luck with sickness among his herd of cattle. Everything was going wrong. Certain that bad spirits had invaded his herd, he turned to his parish priest for help.

The priest, who also believed in spirits, offered to come to the farmer's house. The ritual went like this: First the priest would perform mass in the farmer's small house. At the end of the mass, the farmer was to drive the herd of cattle in through the front door and out the back door. He was to inform the priest when the last cow was passing.

The idea was to dump all the bad luck of the herd onto the last cow. The cow would then be turned into hamburger, and the spell of the bad spirits would be broken.

The farmer chased his cows up to the house and probably had quite a time getting them in the front door. When the last animal was about to enter the house, the farmer had a change of heart. Not wanting to lose the cow, he neglected to call out to the priest that it was the last one. Just as the animal went out the back door, the priest fell over and died.

The storyteller didn't give an explanation for what had happened. I suspect the authors didn't know either. It was simply this: The bad luck actually was the farmer's karma, and the purpose of the ritual was to symbolically transfer his karma to the herd. Had the farmer done his part properly, after the rest of the herd had passed through the house, all the karma would have gone to the last cow. This is similar to what occurred in the time of Jesus when the devils went into the herd of swine.

The belief in this ritual was so strong that when the farmer backed out at the last minute, the karma which would have all gone on the last cow was transferred to the priest. The load was so great that it destroyed him.

Even behind an apparently apocryphal story can lie truth. In this case, someone saw a spiritual principle in operation and put it in parable form.

Karmic Overload

People who do psychic healings are often plagued by karmic overload. They don't know how to be detached about it. They get so emotional about the health of their patients that they find themselves constantly ill.

It happens simply because they do not recognize or understand the Law of Karma. They don't realize that the people who come to them for a healing have earned those illnesses through violation of some spiritual law.

This is not to say that a healer or anyone else should avoid compassion. It means that the way to not take on another person's illness is to have the ability to be detached. So if someone asks you for help, you can give what help you can; or, better yet, turn them over to a professional who is trained in the art of healing.

A medical doctor's training and experience prepare him to be detached when dealing with illness, even if his treatment does not result in a healing. He learns that there is only so much he can do for other people, and then he must let go and allow them to have their own experience.

Self-Discipline in Healing

One example is when a doctor tells a patient: "If you want to get well, you will have to take these pills three times a day for the next four weeks." The doctor knows that from this point on it is up to the patient to implement the instructions.

The patient does it for a day or two, then gets too busy with other things to keep it up. This lack of self-discipline results in a relapse, which means no healing is accomplished.

Now a patient won't automatically be healed just because he listens to his doctor. This is not always the case. The illness is the effect of a particular karmic problem that he incurred for himself. But if the medication were right for him, he might overcome the illness. He could be healed.

But, then, what is life all about? It's learning firsthand about the things that are harmful to us. Yet this knowledge alone is not enough to keep us out of trouble or to keep us from getting ill. We also have to exercise the self-discipline to keep away from the harmful things.

Of course, our rate of success or failure at self-discipline varies. Sometimes we are good at it; other times, not so good. Life allows us the opportunity to learn at our own pace.

Swimming Upstream

As we go farther on our journey home, we develop more of an understanding into life. Before, our solutions generally came from the field of power. Now we turn more often to love and understanding. This often allows the problem to resolve itself.

Many stories come from ECK initiates in Africa. They

have a good understanding of how the Holy Spirit works. They recognize their relationship with the ECK and how to fit in with the flow of life. Instead of constantly resisting it, constantly finding a way to swim upstream, they try to go with the flow of Spirit.

At some point in their unfoldment, most people display a peculiar knack for swimming upstream, while those with spiritual insight are going with the current. This does not mean being wishy-washy. It means knowing when Divine Spirit, or the Mahanta, is giving you direction, recognizing what true direction is, and following it.

The Bee Tree

An ECKist who is a doctor in one of the African countries had just left the hospital where he worked. As he started his walk around the building, which would take him past a fruit tree, one of the nurses came up to him. "Doctor, don't go that way," she said. "There is a cluster of bees in that tree."

Following her pointing finger, he saw what looked like a huge ball attached to the little tree. "The bees came about two days ago," the nurse said. "Everyone at the hospital has been avoiding that path. We are afraid they might sting." There were so many bees that the stings could have been fatal.

As they discussed ways to get rid of the bees, the doctor told her, "When I was a boy, one method I used was to set the grass near the bees on fire and try to smoke them out." Boys have ingenious ways to take care of problems. I know, because I did—and I paid my karmic debt for them.

"There are many things we could do," the doctor continued, "but they all involve using force. That is not necessary. The bees will go when they are ready, and they will leave as quickly as they came. Let's not disturb them now."

He went back in the hospital and returned to work. Five minutes later the nurse came over to him and said, "I should have come to you two days ago, Doctor. You won't believe this, but every bee is gone."

The doctor was surprised too. Even though such experiences often occur in the life of an ECKist, they don't become commonplace. You're still learning. Things don't always work out the same way. Under different conditions, the bees might not have left.

Sending Love

About two months later, just as the doctor arrived at the hospital early in the morning, the same nurse ran up to him to report another problem. "Doctor, an ox has gotten into the hospital compound. What should we do?" She had gained an extra amount of respect for him since the bee incident. She figured he knew something about handling creatures that others did not.

The doctor thought back to his boyhood days, when he would chase away an ox by throwing stones at him. The ox might run away or it might come after you. Either way, you got him to leave the place where he wasn't wanted.

The doctor went to the fenced area where the ox was chewing grass, and picked up some stones. But as he watched the animal, he thought about how he would feel if he were at his breakfast table and somebody came along and threw stones at him. How would he like it? He put the stones back down on the ground.

"What are we going to do about this ox, Doctor?" the nurse asked.

The doctor opened the gate leading out of the hospital compound, then went over and stood near the ox. "Finish your breakfast," he said to the animal. "When you are done, please leave by this gate." With those words, the ox gave a sudden jump, as if it had just received a shock. The doctor stepped back and watched.

The ox went back to eating the grass and continued for about five more minutes. When it was finished, it turned toward the open gate and leisurely made its way out of the compound.

Once again, the nurse was very impressed, and the doctor was greatly surprised. But he didn't let on.

When the ECK is working for you, even if you are not quite sure how It is working, it is best to just keep quiet about it. Otherwise you might start taking credit for it. And as sure as you do, the next time will find you getting stung by the bees or chased by the ox.

That is sometimes what must happen before you learn that it wasn't you at all: It was a power greater than you. And It was able to work through you at a time when you were open to the action of the Light and Sound.

The doctor may not have realized it, but as he spoke to the ox, he was sending it love. This was experienced by the animal as a jolt of some kind. If we can learn to do all things with love, we have come a long way on our journey home.

The Tooth Fairy

An ECKist's six-year-old son, unlike his friends, had been taught not to believe in the Tooth Fairy. One day a friend of his, younger by a year, ran up to him and proudly waved his first baby tooth in the air.

"Look at this!" he squealed. "I got no tooth! I'm growing up!" When a second friend came over and grinned widely to show off the gap in his mouth, the little ECKist began to feel bad. His friends were on the threshold of something great, and he was being left behind.

As soon as he got home he asked his mother, "Mommy, when am I gonna lose my teeth? Michael and Ryan are losing theirs."

"Don't worry about it," his mother said. "When the time is right, the new teeth will grow in underneath your baby teeth and push them out. It will happen very naturally."

A few weeks later, the great event occurred when the little boy bit into an apple. The experience stirred up mixed feelings in him. On the one hand, he had a sense of loss, because he really didn't want to be without his teeth. On the other hand, it meant that he was growing up. He was on his way to being a big boy now.

"Will the Tooth Fairy come tonight?" he asked his mother.

"You know better than that," she said. "I told you before: I'm Santa Claus; I'm the Tooth Fairy." Most children know that early on, but they try to keep the game going for as long as possible. Why? Because there's a benefit to believing in the Tooth Fairy. It brings good things. And as long as they can convince their parents that they still believe, so much the better.

The boy persisted. "I want to put the tooth under my pillow so the Tooth Fairy will bring me a present."

"No," his mother said. She didn't have time for such silly games. There were two younger children to take care of, and she was just too busy.

"Please, Mommy?"

"No!"

"Please?"

"OK." She was melting now. "You can put it in an envelope and leave it next to your pillow."

"Thanks!" He was so relieved. He went to bed happy, knowing that the Tooth Fairy would come while he was asleep.

The mother forgot all about the tooth. To her the Tooth Fairy was a meaningless ritual. After all, she was an ECKist, and she tried to teach her son not to be fooled by illusions of this nature.

At two o'clock in the morning, her younger son began to cry. The mother quickly jumped up and went to get him settled down before his crying woke up the other children. In the bedroom she saw the envelope next to her six-year-old son's pillow and was reminded of the tooth. Since she was the one who told him to leave it out, she figured she had better do something about it.

Carefully lifting the envelope from the bed, she took it into the kitchen. There she removed the tooth and replaced it with two oatmeal cookies. She also wrote out a note on a blue piece of paper, stating that it was a ticket good for one movie with buttered popcorn. She then sealed the envelope and placed it back on his bed.

The next morning the boy came running out of his room with the envelope. "Mommy, look! The Tooth Fairy came!" She didn't say anything to diminish his joy. It was a silly game, but it was nice to see him so happy.

"Mommy, what does it say on this blue paper?" She read him the note: a movie and buttered popcorn that afternoon. He was so excited! He immediately ran off to tell his younger brother and sister, "Hey, look what the Tooth Fairy brought me!" Later, as his mother was going about her housework, she overheard him thanking God for letting his mom let him have the Tooth Fairy.

Any child who really believes in this game knows that once the Tooth Fairy leaves something in place of the tooth, the trade is complete—the tooth is gone for good.

157

But this little boy knew both sides of the story.

"Mommy, where's the tooth?" he asked. But he whispered it very quietly, just in case the Tooth Fairy was nearby. You can never be completely sure about these things. "In the cupboard," she said. So he gathered the tooth, his cookies, and his blue ticket, and went out to show his friends that he was every bit as grown up as they were.

He also got to show it to Grandpa, Grandma, and all the other relatives. He was actually enjoying the best of both worlds: A present from the Tooth Fairy without really having to believe in it. On top of that, he got his tooth back, so he was able to get even more mileage out of it. And now, of course, his younger brother and sister eagerly awaited their turn with the Tooth Fairy.

The mother realized something from her son's happiness over this apparently empty ritual. He now fit in with his friends. He felt like one of the gang. Even though he knew that the Tooth Fairy was a myth, he wouldn't have to stand apart from the others, and that made it so much easier for him at school. Because the mother loved her son, she was able to see this and to play the game with him.

A Greater Person

From time to time, we all find ourselves in the position of doing something that we would rather not do, but we do it anyway, out of love. Occasionally an ECKist is asked to attend church with his family, for instance. He may not want to go, but he does it because it means a lot to the people he loves. It isn't as if the minister is going to tie Soul to the church bell, and zip! It's lost. If your strength in ECK can be lost in a visit to church to make your family happy, then your trust is pretty weak and probably wouldn't last very long anyway.

The story about the Tooth Fairy also shows that sometimes we do things to be part of society. We don't have to do them, but sometimes it's selfish not to. Maybe doing things for others—such as going to church with the family only because it makes them happy—makes one a greater person. If there is a bond of love between the people, what difference does it make whether a Catholic comes to an ECK function or an ECKist goes to a Catholic mass?

What the mother learned from her son is that the most important substance of any experience is love.

Wave of Love

After an ECK initiate's grandmother translated, or died, he felt a strong desire to see her one more time. In contemplation one evening, he said to the Mahanta, who is known as Wah Z on the inner planes, "I would like to be with my grandmother, if I could."

He soon found himself in one of the inner worlds, looking out over a calm, serene ocean. Off in the distance there appeared a sailboat with three people. As it sailed to shore, he saw that the ECK Master Rebazar Tarzs was at the tiller. Wah Z was seated, and beside him was the initiate's grandmother.

The ECKist waded out to meet the boat. "Grandmother," he said, "is it all right if I go with you a little ways on your journey?"

"Sure," she said.

He got in the boat, grateful to have this chance to be with her. After they talked for a while, he said, "Grandmother, I have to go back now."

"All right," she said. "Give Grandfather my love, and tell him that I'll be waiting for him."

As he was driving to work the next day, the ECKist

suddenly felt an incredible wave of love wash over him. It lasted for about ten minutes, during which time he strongly felt the presence of the Mahanta and his grandmother.

His grandmother's death had been very hard on the family. When the ECKist told them of his experience—that he had sailed with her on the inner planes in the presence of two ECK Masters—they listened with interest. It gave them consolation. It lightened their grief to hear that these Masters of compassion and kindness were there to help those who were traveling this leg of the journey home to God.

After he finished telling them of his inner experience, the initiate's mother, who was a Christian, was silent for a moment. Finally she said to him, "I'm going to ask the Mahanta to please be with Mother on her journey home."

The family was comforted to have this confirmation that death was not a fearsome thing, nor final. There are many people not in ECK who are ready to know about the journey home to God by the way of ECK.

HU to the God Worlds

I would like to mention again the spiritual exercise that was covered briefly last night. It is a creative technique that starts with the imagination. It takes you on an inner journey through the lower worlds, and up to the Soul Plane.

In contemplation, slowly chant the word *HU*, the Holy name of God, five times. With the first HU, imagine yourself on the Astral Plane. Even if you have no idea of what images to use, just know you are there. Don't worry about results.

Chant HU the second time, and this takes you to the Causal Plane. This is the plane of memories of past lives.

Then chant the third HU, which brings you to the Mental Plane. This is the area of great concepts and ideas, where the individual reaches the source of phenomenal mental abilities.

The fourth chanting of HU takes you to the Etheric Plane, the area of the unconscious, or subconscious, mind. This is a high sheath of the mind. It is the last covering of Soul in the lower worlds, before It reaches the Soul Plane.

The fifth HU, then, brings you to the Soul Plane—the first of the true worlds of the Light and Sound of God.

May the blessings be.

ECK Springtime Seminar, Anaheim, California, Saturday, April 2, 1988

It takes spiritual sight to see that when life brings us a problem, it also brings the answer. We could save ourselves a lot of worry if we remembered this.

10

So How Does the ECK Work?

One ECKist has been serving as an ECK missionary in his business travels to the Far East. Other initiates, too, are learning the adventure and joy of presenting the ECK message to those who want to hear it.

Vehicles for ECK

Whether in my position or yours, none of us controls the ECK. We simply act as vehicles to carry out to the best of our abilities what the ECK wants done.

This is what it means to be a channel for ECK. We do what seems best, knowing that it is not us who is doing it. Everything runs smoothly, as long as we realize that it is the ECK, the greater power of Divine Spirit, working through us.

Sometimes, after things go well for a while, we begin to get a big head. Little by little, we start to take credit for the workings of the ECK. Because of this, very gradually things will take a turn and begin to go wrong. And since we thought we were the ones making it all work so well in the first place, we question why it is now going wrong.

Out on a Limb

When the ECK doesn't respond—having gone in Its own direction, to get things done some other way—we feel we are out on a limb all by ourself. Then we begin to complain—the ECK doesn't work, the Master has forgotten me, and so on.

This will change for the better only when we come to the realization that, at the same time we began to take credit, we also began to depend less on the ECK.

Connecting ECKists

An initiate who travels to give ECK introductory presentations made an interesting discovery. Often, the people who show up already know each other from business or their neighborhood. But until they came to the ECK talk, they didn't know their acquaintances were ECKists too.

Introductory presentations are not just for people new to ECK. They also put the ECKists in touch with each other. As this individual travels, serving as a channel for the ECK by giving talks, he is also acting as a channel to cement the bond of fellowship between the ECKists. Those on the path of ECK know the love of Spirit and appreciate the bond of love with fellow initiates.

The Cat and the Hamsters

A family has a big black cat named Lucky, who is a very good hunter. Many mornings the mother opens the front door to find that the cat has brought her a mouse, sometimes half a mouse. In his own way, Lucky is bringing her a gift of love.

As the family was getting ready to leave for a camping trip, the mother made careful preparations for the family pets. First, she made sure that the door to the children's room was tightly shut so the cat couldn't get in to eat their two hamsters. Then she put Lucky's litter box and plenty of cat food in the usual place outside the children's room. The final step was to bring the cat into the house and let him know they were leaving. But no matter where they looked, Lucky was nowhere to be found.

When pets feel left out, they often go off and hide. Since this often happened before a trip, nobody worried about it. When the family got home two days later, the first sound they heard was the cat's loud meowing. Relief was quickly replaced by worry when they noticed that it was coming from the children's room.

The mother realized that Lucky had been hiding in there before they left. When she shut the door to keep him out, the cat had actually been locked in with the hamsters and away from his food for the entire weekend.

She didn't have the courage to open the door. But her young children bolted straight for the door, flung it open, and found the hamsters alive and in good health. The big black cat was sitting there quietly, very hungry from two days with no food.

The family had given a lot of love to Lucky, and the cat had observed them giving the same kind of love to the hamsters. He was able to understand that they too were pets, not food. Because there was an abundance of love, even animals normally in danger from a hungry predator were safe.

This is an example of the protection of the ECK, but it doesn't always work the same way. I wouldn't advise anyone to experiment by leaving their hungry cat in a room with the hamster or canary. The cat may not feel particularly loving that day.

Reading Glasses

One morning an ECK couple were having breakfast together before the wife left for work. The husband, who had the day off, planned to spend it at home. The wife ate quickly and rushed out the door, saying that she had to stop at the post office on her way to work.

As soon as she drove off, the husband noticed that she had left her reading glasses on the table. He knew she would be upset when she discovered she had forgotten them, because she wouldn't be able to do her work. But since he had no car that day, he didn't know how he could help.

He had often heard other ECKists talk about the inner communication that exists between people who love each other and love the Mahanta. This seemed like a good time to give it a try. He sat down, closed his eyes, and attempted to send a mental message to his wife: "You left your reading glasses at home. Please come back and get them."

But a mental command doesn't have the power of the spiritual voice, which is picked up instantly through the direct perception of Soul. Mind is slower than Soul; mind often runs into blocks when trying to transmit or receive messages, even between loved ones. The man could sense that his message was not getting through to his wife.

He closed his eyes once more, but this time he did not try to send any messages. Instead, he went into contemplation and thought of nothing except the love that he had for his wife. He concluded by saying to the Mahanta, the Inner Master, "Give my love to my wife."

A few minutes later he heard a car pull into the driveway. He looked out the window and saw that it was his wife. This was unexpected—he thought she would be well on her way to work by now. As she came in the door he said, "Did you know that you forgot your reading glasses?"

"No," she said, giving him a surprised look. "I just decided to bring you some newspapers to read, so you'd have something to do during the day."

The underlying element here was love—for SUGMAD, the ECK, and the Mahanta. There was also a deep love for someone who was precious and dear. He was trying to reach her because he loved her, and she responded to the love by going out of her way to bring him the newspapers. Love was the factor that enabled them to communicate with each other through the invisible lines of communication.

The ECK works this way in the daily lives of many ECK initiates. There is inner communication between the ECKists, and the connecting link is always love. Because there is a bond of love, the ECK can work.

Understanding the Loving Heart

If the ECK doesn't seem to be working in your life, perhaps it is because you have yet to come to a greater understanding of the loving heart. This is what allows you to love something more than you love yourself.

There is nothing wrong with loving yourself. In fact, you have to love yourself spiritually, even as you would love God, before you can love anyone or anything else.

Many ECKists came from religious backgrounds which said to love God, when they didn't really love themselves. They were expected to practice all kinds of austerities to prove their love for God. They somehow thought they would be most loved by God if they were needy, poor, and contrite. After all, they were corrupt from birth, weren't they?

What a burden to carry through life—that you are damned from birth. This is one of the greatest perversions to come out of any religious teaching.

In ECK our teaching is this: Soul is a creation of God sent into the lower worlds for experience. As Soul gains experience through the ups and downs of life, eventually It will reach the point where It may join the ranks of the saints or the Masters, to become a Co-worker with God.

In other words, in ECK we recognize inexperience; we do not recognize the concept of total depravity of the individual. And there is a difference. All experience, whether good or bad, is always leading us home to God.

Finally, as we become filled with the love of ECK, we live, breathe, and move in ECK. Every act we perform is weighed and tempered with, "What can I do at this particular moment that will be best for my spiritual unfoldment?"

To keep this in mind at all times may seem like a difficult feat. But those who move along the path into the high initiations do eventually become aware, every moment, of their bond of love with Divine Spirit. With this awareness, the outer events of their life begin to change; they treat their fellowman in a different way.

Being an Honest Guy

An ECKist had put off filling his gas tank. One afternoon, shortly after lunch, he noticed that the needle on the gas gauge rested on empty. Though he was running late, he had no choice but to stop at the gas station.

"Fill it up, please," he told the attendant. "As long as I'm here, I might as well get a car wash too."

The attendant poked along, taking his time to fill the tank, clean the windshield, and check the oil. Now that the noon-hour rush was over, he had all the time in the world. When he finally finished all that, he told the ECKist the amount, took his money, and strolled off to get the change. Then he leisurely made his way back and handed the ECKist some bills and coins.

The ECKist took a quick glance at the coins, saw that the amount was correct, and stuck them in his pocket. He was in too much of a hurry to count the bills, so he laid them on the passenger seat and drove around to the car wash at the back of the station.

Sitting in his car as it went through the wash cycle, he counted out the rest of the money and found that the attendant had given him the wrong amount. He had been given too much change—nine dollars too much.

His mind immediately shifted into the game-playing mode: You don't have to return the money, it's legally yours. You've been a loyal customer, and this car wash has always been overpriced, anyway.

These arguments sounded pretty good, until a picture flashed through his mind. It had to do with a story he'd once heard about Abraham Lincoln walking miles to return a penny to the rightful owner.

After he was through in the car wash, the ECKist drove around to the front of the station. "You gave me too much change," he told the attendant, handing him the extra nine dollars.

A product of these cynical times, the attendant reacted with suspicion. "You were in such a big hurry a little while ago," he said. "Are you trying to tell me now that you decided to spend your lunch hour being an honest guy?"

"No," the ECKist said. "That's how I spend my whole life." The words leaped from his lips as if someone else were speaking them, and he knew they came from somewhere higher than his mind.

The attendant studied him closely, looking for signs of his own cynicism. But all he saw in the face of the ECKist was love and understanding. Slowly he began to realize that this customer's honesty had saved him from having to pay the money out of his own pocket at the end of the day. His expression softened, his mood turned happy, and he smiled as they wished each other a good day.

The ECKist saw that his actions had brought upliftment and a change of attitude to another person. It's not that he was trying to change someone else, but his own spiritual code of behavior had made an impression.

When Life Brings a Problem

Sometimes the ECK works to help us out of situations that we get ourselves into. The ECK is always present and ready to offer Its help, but the help comes faster when we can remember to stay relaxed. It is usually during times of anxiety that we forget to relax and stay open to the Mahanta and the ECK. It takes spiritual sight to see that when life brings us a problem, it also brings the answer. We could save ourselves a lot of worry if we remembered this.

A man and his wife were going on a two-day trip. Being one of those people who has several hiding places around the house to foil burglars, the husband tried to decide where to put certain valuable materials before he left.

None of his usual places seemed quite safe enough. "They'll find it too easily," he complained to his wife. He went from room to room, until finally he discovered a brand-new place he was sure no burglar would ever think to look. Quickly stashing the materials, he finished preparing for the trip.

The hiding place was so good that when he got back home two days later, he couldn't remember where it was. Since he hadn't shown his wife, she could not help. He spent the better part of the next two days searching all over the house. The stuff was someplace, but he couldn't figure out where.

On the second night, as he sat relaxing in front of the TV, it occurred to him that he had not done his spiritual exercises since he got home. The search for the lost materials had taken up so much time and energy that he had forgotten his spiritual exercises.

With the TV blaring out the latest news, he closed his eyes and allowed himself to let go of all tension. Soon he was in contemplation. All of a sudden an image flashed in front of his Spiritual Eye. He clearly saw the secret hiding place that contained his valuable possessions.

Only when he was able to stop pushing did he realize that his anxiety had gotten in the way of his spiritual exercises. Because he acted on this realization, the Mahanta was able to show him what he was looking for. There is generally a lesson behind every experience, but until we realize what it is, the situation cannot resolve itself.

Blue Light of ECK

A woman from the United Kingdom and her husband had gone on holiday to visit relatives in Australia. While they were there, the couple went on a sight-seeing tour of some caves. The tour guide was a friendly, informative young fellow. As he took the group through the caves, he pointed out all the marvelous rock formations. He explained that the caverns were formed over thousands of years by water rushing through and eroding the rocks.

The rocks in one of the caves glittered like gold dust. She and her husband found it a spectacular sight.

"Before we leave this cave," the tour guide said, "I want to do a little experiment." He shut off all the lights, leaving the group in total darkness. No one made a sound.

171

"Put your hand two inches in front of your face," he said, to demonstrate to the group that they could see absolutely nothing. Then he said, "Listen and look for anything that you can perceive while the lights are out."

As the cave remained in darkness for about two minutes, the woman saw the Blue Light of ECK. It came as a patch of blue light where there was no natural or artificial illumination. At the same time, she heard a soft humming, which is one of the sounds of ECK.

The tour guide finally turned on the lights, but he didn't ask what they had experienced. The ECKist thought this was strange. She suspected the others may have seen and heard something too. The guide apparently assumed that it was just too dark to see; the only thing to be heard was the sound of blood pumping through your own veins.

If he had bothered to ask if the group had seen or heard anything, he might have been surprised. But because he didn't have the awareness, he didn't ask. He was so sure of his own perceptions that he did not even consider that anyone else's could be different.

I try not to make the teachings of ECK seem so exclusive that it sounds like only those in ECK can see the Light or hear the Sound. That's not true. Many people may experience these manifestations of the Holy Spirit, but without knowing what it means. In ECK we understand their significance in our spiritual life.

People not familiar with the teachings of the Light and Sound might perceive the experience as a mental aberration. They are so wrong, of course, but they don't know it, and there is no one in their circle who can enlighten them.

172

A Life for God

There was an initiate in ECK who worked very hard to present the message of ECK. Besides giving ECK presentations and serving in a leadership position, she was also attending college at night to finish up some courses.

One evening after class, she sat alone in a coffee shop and looked the situation over. Maybe I'm not serving the ECK and the Mahanta by being a student, she thought. Maybe I'm being selfish. Instead of going through the hassle of trying to balance my studies and my ECK activities, maybe I could serve God better by quitting school.

An acquaintance of hers, who was involved in metaphysical studies, came over and asked if he could join her. "Sure," she said. As soon as he sat down, he began to tell her what an inspiration she was to him and others. A love and strength seemed to emanate from her, and they noticed it.

"Actually, what you're feeling is the love of Divine Spirit and the Mahanta," she said. Because he was interested, she went on to tell him more about ECK.

After they had talked for a while, he said, "I can tell you're wondering whether you should quit your studies and devote more of your time to your path." He then said something that put the situation in perspective for her: "If you would consider your studies as a part of your life for God and integrate it all into one whole unit, you'd find that everything would work out well for you."

He had to leave then, but she stayed for a while longer and thought about what had just taken place. She was in ECK, had been willing to bring the Light and Sound to others, and knew that the Mahanta was always with her. Even so, the burdens of life had seemed heavy enough to make her wonder if she was doing the right thing.

This is when the young man had come to her. Though not an ECK initiate, he had been touched by the love of the Mahanta coming through her. He was able to return it by giving her good counsel. She now knew that there was a way to make her college studies a valuable part of her spiritual life.

She realized then that this "chance meeting" had been arranged by the Mahanta. When she was down, the Master had sent another Soul to give her the encouragement she needed to get back up.

Mahanta Transcripts

We've just released *Journey of Soul,* the first of the Mahanta transcripts. These are edited versions of talks I have given at ECK seminars. They include many stories that I hope will be helpful to you.

Listening to a talk is one way to gain knowledge, but some people can absorb more by reading. If there is a point you want to think about, you can put the book down. You can take whatever time you need without missing anything else.

Show Time

We also plan to present a play based on "Show Time," a chapter from Phil Morimitsu's book *In the Company of ECK Masters.*

Some people are sensitive to the way Jesus is portrayed in "Show Time." Combining certain ECK principles, it shows him in a different light than the orthodox view. Realize, though, if there weren't already many different views of Christ within Christianity, there would not be so many different sects.

The story is not intended to be insensitive to the beliefs of Christians, but I realize to some people the criticisms may appear to be valid. Taking this into consideration, I had to decide if this was a time to put truth in perspective.

Just because a certain religion has a mistaken notion about the Law of Karma or anything else, it doesn't mean we should not express our views. It would be irresponsible for me to ignore the issue. There is nothing to be gained by trying to make believe that we are in total harmony with other religious teachings or other spiritual beliefs. The reason there are so many different religions on earth is because people do not all share the same beliefs—and we in ECK are no exception. This is why we have our own teachings.

Consciousness in the world has reached a point where there can be such a variance of beliefs. It is commendable that we no longer have to fear religious wars whenever we express our beliefs to someone who doesn't agree with them.

Upward Movement in Consciousness

Show Time has an important place in presenting the ECK message at this particular time. It may offend some people, of course. Remember what happened when *Jesus Christ, Superstar* first came out? While the movie pulled people upward in consciousness, there was also quite a violent reaction from many in the Christian community. This is what occurs whenever there an upward movement in consciousness. But as people got used to seeing Jesus as more of a human being, it stopped being such a big deal.

Though some people may be upset by *Show Time,* I also think the consciousness in general has expanded to the point where they may not be as sensitive as we imagine.

175

There is only one way to find out, and that is by experience. That's why we are on the path of ECK.

Walk the Path

If you are in doubt about something and suspect that a spiritual end can be achieved by it, then do it and find out. It's a lot better than sitting back and wondering, How would that have turned out? If you do it, you'll know.

Life consists of two roads—the one where you do something and the one where you don't. As for the road not taken, you can only speculate on what it might have been like. So if you are really curious about something in life, or you feel that there may be some great spiritual benefit for you by walking a certain path, walk that path and find out.

A Spiritual Reunion

ECK seminars are really spiritual reunions. That is why we come back to them again and again. The ECK community is a good reflection of life in today's mobile society, in which families move an average of once every four years. Sometimes the only place to see the friends you've made in a particular area is at an ECK seminar, and so I think of our gatherings as ECK reunions.

As you make your way home, I would like to wish you the love of the SUGMAD, the ECK, and the Mahanta.

ECK Springtime Seminar, Anaheim, California,
Sunday, April 3, 1988

The eternal dreamer starts to see himself more clearly, and often he doesn't like what he sees. He can then either resist who he is or—better yet—he can accept who he is.

11

The Eternal Dreamer, Part 1

Eternal in the true sense means not being limited by time or space. The eternal dreamer obtains his experiences both here in the physical world as well as in the inner worlds.

I research the dream state in an effort to find a thread of common experience for the eternal dreamer. My research has barely begun. It doesn't begin to cover all the different areas that the dreamer may encounter as he travels the path of ECK.

Eight Types of Dreams

Though we do not put too much attention on interpreting dream symbology, there really is nothing wrong with this. It can be a step in our own unfoldment. However, in ECK we put a different slant on the subject than is found in psychology or through other sources: We learn to identify the different areas of the dream life as they relate to our own spiritual life.

There are eight categories of dreams that I would like to discuss. Examples will be given to help you recognize them, both in the waking state and during the sleep state. You can then try to see how they advance your own spiritual understanding. The list is not complete, but it will serve as a starting point in learning the ECK definition of what happens in your own dream world.

The eight categories are (1) daydreams; (2) initiation dreams; (3) dreams of intrusion; (4) dreams of release from fear; (5) the waking dream; (6) the Golden-tongued Wisdom, which is part of the ancient science of prophecy, the ECK-Vidya; (7) dreams of understanding; and (8) dreams with the Mahanta, which include experiences with the Light and Sound—the essence of the ECK teachings.

Looking Closely

Yesterday I had to sit through a photo session, which I do not particularly like. The photographs are for use in the ECK Centers, to give the initiates a focus for their contemplation. The current ones are four years old, so it was time for an update.

A photographer pointed out that people are reluctant to have their pictures taken because they don't like to see the aging. I understood what he meant.

A photograph cuts through the illusion of who and what we are. Like it or not, we get to look at ourselves a bit more honestly than we do in the mirror, and this cracks our personal image of how we appear to other people.

The eternal dreamer starts to see himself more clearly, and often he doesn't like what he sees. He can then either resist who he is or—better yet—accept who he is. This is when he can say, "I am what I am, and I will be that with as much grace as I can muster at this time."

Spiritual Influence

One of the ECK initiates wrote a book which is slated to be picked up by the Writer's Digest Book Club. The ECK writers, artists, musicians, playwrights, and actors are finding new ways to develop their talents.

Through the inspiration they have gained in ECK, these initiates are carrying the ECK message in some form to the world. They convey the spiritual principles without using the ECK terms when it's more appropriate not to use them. Nor do they proclaim, "This is an ECK principle. I am applying it, and now I do things better."

Instead, the ECKists in all these different fields are beginning to incorporate the ECK principles in their work in a very natural way. I am happy that they are finding their way into bigger areas of spiritual influence.

A Slight Case of Vanity

A play entitled *Show Time* was adapted from a chapter of the book *In the Company of ECK Masters* by Phil Morimitsu. As the script was being written, one of my concerns was that the role of Jesus be treated with respect. The message he brought two thousand years ago has uplifted many people spiritually. I felt we ought to show some deference to the service provided by this messenger, who was also of the SUGMAD.

Some of the ECKists become very possessive of those in the line of ECK Mastership. They discount the reality of the other masters. Keep in mind that Jesus and others were teachers who brought people along the spiritual path from other directions.

It's easy to become egotistical and develop a slight case of vanity when it comes to our own religious path. But as we know from history, such vanity, when carried to an extreme, can lead to suppression of other paths. This is especially true when the numbers and power of one particular group become greater than that of the others.

We too have to be careful of that. A good time to start is while the students of the ECK teachings are still in the minority. We can set a good example by showing respect for the teachers of other religious paths.

Even so, we must point out the weaknesses within certain teachings, especially if we see a void where there should be Light and Sound. It is similar to the responsibility you feel when you see a child breaking a lamp. Whether it was done through ignorance, carelessness, or willfulness, you have an obligation to somehow point out the error of his ways. But it doesn't mean you love him any less.

Daydream of Editor-in-Chief

I read a story in *Writer's Digest* about a writer who diligently plugged away at his craft. Every day he wrote and wrote, but he didn't sell much. He practiced every technique he felt a successful writer would use: When he found a topic of interest, he'd research it, write an article, and mail it to a publisher.

After eighteen months, he tallied up his earnings. They amounted to only seven thousand dollars—a long way from being enough to support himself and his family.

Totally dejected, he sat back in his chair. Soon he was involved in a daydream in which he was the editor-in-chief of a large New York magazine. From this top position in the organization, he began an inner dialogue: "You know, this magazine could use a few articles." All of a sudden, with an amazing degree of clarity, he saw all the different subjects that the readers of the magazine would like.

Snapping out of his daydream, he picked up a pencil and made a list of all these topics. He selected one to start with, then reviewed past issues of the magazine. Sure enough, the subject had not been covered: How to get a cab in New York City when you want one.

He did some quick research and gathered information from cab companies. After he wrote an outline of his ideas, he called the magazine. "Would you be interested in an article about what to do when you need a cab in Manhattan?" he asked one of the editors.

The editor was not only interested, he was willing to work with the writer to develop the article. When it was completed, the magazine bought it for several thousand dollars—all for one story.

He no longer limits his writing to subjects *he* thinks are important. Instead, he has learned to assume the viewpoint of the person who knows what the readers want. He went on to write many other articles for major magazines, and his financial picture improved greatly. Through his daydream, he found a way to build a successful career for himself.

Initiation Dreams

The First Initiation in ECK comes in the dream state. It generally happens within six months to a year after one begins to study the ECK discourses. This is when the individual meets the Mahanta, the Inner Master, on the inner planes. Whether he remembers the experience or not, this is an important point in his spiritual life.

One ECKist reported this dream. He was a child playing in the street with friends. The setting was tropical, much like Hawaii.

Suddenly he looked up and saw the Mahanta coming down the street. As the Master walked past, he looked directly at the dreamer. The Master then entered a nearby house. The dreamer was close enough to watch him pick

183

up the phone, dial a number, and carry on a conversation.

All the while, the Master's gaze never left the dreamer. Finally the Master hung up the phone, nodded and smiled at the dreamer, and walked away.

The ECKist awoke with the memory fresh in his mind, and he immediately realized the importance of the experience. Through the image of making a call on the inner planes, the Inner Master was letting him know that the connection had been made with the ECK. The Mahanta had made the linkup between the chela and the ECK, the Holy Spirit. This initiate was fortunate; sometimes one cannot even put into words the realization that comes with the initiation experience.

While the First Initiation in ECK takes place entirely in the dream state, the Second through Eighth initiations occur in two parts. The first part comes on the inner planes, and some time after that an ECK Initiator, acting as a channel for the Mahanta, gives the outer initiation.

Dreams of Intrusion

To understand this category of dreams, we must assume the viewpoint of the dreamer, whether asleep or daydreaming.

Let's say you are having a dream in which a certain friend, love interest, relative, or other acquaintance appears. Normally any of these people would show up in your dreams in a predictable way, acting pretty much the same as they do in their everyday life.

But all of a sudden you have a dream experience where things are topsy-turvy; the people are acting out of character. This could be a sign that someone—whether close to you or outside your circle—is unconsciously projecting his or her thoughts into your dream world. This is a dream of intrusion.

If that person has an aberration of some kind, or perhaps thinks of you as a playboy or playgirl, those feelings may be projected into your dream state and affect the actions of the characters in your dream. Naturally you are going to wonder what is going on. If misunderstood, it could cause jealousy and other problems in the outer world.

For instance, say an old girlfriend of the dreamer has been thinking about him a lot, unconsciously wanting to break up his new relationship. Her thoughts and hopes intrude in his dream life. When the dreamer wakes up, he misinterprets the dream and says, "My current girl-friend is not being faithful to me—I've seen it on the inner planes." And so jealousy arises.

If you have a dream in which someone who has shown up repeatedly in the past is suddenly acting out of char-acter, look for certain traits. Then look around you in the physical world. There may be someone who either has those traits or, more likely, imagines that you have those traits. Through this method, you may be able to identify the person who has been sending these signals into your dream world.

Putting Up a Screen

What do you do now? Do you confront the person and accuse them of sending you psychic attacks? Frankly, it is a cop-out to put the responsibility for our inner worlds on other people. Even if somebody is able to transmit or broadcast a wrong signal into your dream life, it is your responsibility to shut it off at this end. The only reason they are able to get in is because somehow, in some way, you haven't put up a screen to stop that kind of intrusion.

The creative part of the eternal dreamer must figure out a way to do this without causing problems out here in the physical world. This can be tricky. But imagine what would happen if you went up to the person and spouted off: "You have been intruding in my dreams. I want you to get out and never come back!" He would be completely astounded. He wouldn't know what you were talking about. Since he is working from the unconscious level, he probably has no idea that he is invading your space.

If it becomes a problem, you can begin to cut back your contact with that person. This includes meetings, phone calls, and correspondence. The way to protect yourself is to begin shutting down the pipeline of negativity that is being fed into you.

In Charge of Your Dream

Another kind of dream of intrusion can cause you, the dreamer, to lose confidence in yourself. Usually you are in charge of what is happening in your dream world, just as you are out here. When you're cleaning your house, you don't have someone else telling you how to do it. In other words, you are not the servant in your own home.

But occasionally you might have a dream in which there is a turnabout of roles. Throughout the entire experience, you seem to be behind the eight ball. Someone else is telling you how to do this, how to do that. No matter what you do, it's wrong. Before you finish a certain task, they'll say, "Let so-and-so do it—he can do it better." If you make a suggestion, one of your dream characters will say how foolish it is.

By the time you wake up in the morning, your security and self-confidence are shattered. Doubts about your ability set in. You begin to wonder if you're really as good at your job as you thought. You can't seem to make decisions with your full creative power. You are in a reactive mode, almost apologetic about whatever you say or do.

186

And you won't get any help from those around you, either. Sensing that you are in this reactive, apologetic mode, they become like healthy fish in an aquarium with the sick fish: they give absolutely no mercy. All this happens simply because someone with a negative opinion about how you live your life or do your job has intruded into your dream.

The solution, again, is to try to trace the attitudes that are being expressed during this dream of intrusion. Then use your inner direction to find out who among your acquaintances has a similar attitude about you.

Teaching You Strength

Once you know who is rewriting your dream script to impose their own disturbing thoughts into your inner worlds, take precautionary measures. Watch your conversations around this person or group of people. Start backing off from being friends with them.

As much as you can, keep away from people who disrupt your life. They can only do it because at this time you do not have the strength, the force field of love, or the spiritual stamina to overcome their intrusion.

Rather than being all bad, these dreams of intrusion teach you to become a stronger individual. You grow more aware of the sources of such attempts to dethrone you. This is essentially what is happening: Someone is trying to dethrone you from your spiritual position. Whether or not you allow this is up to you.

Keep in mind that you are always led into a higher state of challenge. When you become strong enough to face one level of obstacles or intrusions, the ECK raises you to the next level. Once again, you have to figure out how to meet the greater challenges.

God from the Sky

When handling a dream of intrusion or some other complicated situation, life can seem like a poorly written play. The ancient Greek playwrights used a tactic known as *deus ex machina*—god from a machine. Another way of saying it is *god from the sky*.

The writer creates a drama around a character. The character performs all sorts of heroic feats. At some point, the writer paints his hero into a corner and doesn't know how to get him out. The solution? Have a deity swoop down from the sky—by way of stage machinery—pick up the hero, and take him away to safety.

Instead of having the character figure his own way out of the situation, the writer brings in a celestial being to rescue him. Nowadays this would be considered poor plotting.

Whenever I watch an episode of the old *Star Trek* TV series, I look for some element of *deus ex machina*.

A recurring theme finds the starship *Enterprise* rushing through space to a specific destination. Suddenly a call for help comes in from some planet off the beaten track. The problem is, if the *Enterprise* doesn't reach the original destination on schedule, there will be a great catastrophe in the universes.

Captain Kirk makes his decision: "We will go off course and find out what's happening on this out-of-the-way planet." He and other crew members then proceed to the transporter room, where they are beamed down to the planet. And in record time, all communication with the *Enterprise* is cut off.

So Captain Kirk and the others are trapped on this planet, captive of either enemy aliens or some mysterious force. How will they ever get themselves out of this fix?

This is where I watch for the writers to cheat. Before

Captain Kirk can figure a way out of the problem with the tools at hand, will a rescuer suddenly beam down and blast the bad guys away? In most of the episodes I have seen, the writers don't take the easy way out. They make the crew work out a solution even before the starship reestablishes communication with them.

This is my point: The Mahanta should not be routinely treated as the *deus ex machina*.

Your Life's Script

Sometimes your life seems to flow like a well-written script. You can handle the storyline. If a problem arises, you can solve it by yourself. It's your story, you're the star, everything's going great, and the world loves you.

Then you come to a chapter that seems to have been devised by a very poor scriptwriter. Problems come up with your health, personal relationships, job, finances, or anything of this nature. All of a sudden, you can't handle it. This is when you say, "Mahanta, help me!"

Develop Your Creativity

There is nothing wrong with asking for help, but we must remember that our purpose for being on earth is to learn how to arrive at the correct solution to our own problems. We have to write the script and—as well as we can—figure out how to untangle the plot.

If we can't get ourselves out of the fix, there is always *deus ex machina*. This divine intervention is a true, spiritual quality of the teachings of ECK. It is the essential element.

An equally essential part of the teachings is to develop your creativity. Then you can learn to resolve your own problems. Remember, they are problems that you have made for yourself. Out of the factors that made these problems, surely there must be solutions.

An initiate wrote to say that he was very upset when I described the heavens. I said they were still evolving. I was referring to the lower worlds—the Astral, Causal, Mental, and Etheric Planes. From the Soul Plane on up are worlds beyond the knowledge of the orthodox religions. They actually are beyond eternity.

This person took issue over my comment that heaven was a prototype for what we find here on earth in our everyday life. "I prefer a heaven where the people walk around in long robes," he insisted. All I can say is, if he wants his heaven like that, I don't mind. In fact, if he wants to walk around down here in a long robe, that's OK too.

Evolutionary Process

As I travel the inner planes, occasionally I return to places I haven't visited for thirty years. I see wonderful and sometimes strange things. But mostly I see the continuing evolutionary process.

Many years ago I journeyed to a city that had the flavor of an old-fashioned small town. The population has increased since then, and the people have had to make adjustments. The downtown area has been restructured into a mall. The main street is closed to traffic now; there are rows and rows of bicycle racks. Cars have to be left in an area beyond the immediate downtown section. I found these changes interesting.

I went into the bank to deposit some money. A very proper woman sat stiffly on a high stool in the teller's cage. Workmen drifted in and out, repairing some kind of a machine that hasn't manifested on the physical plane. Everything in the bank still looked old-fashioned except for this machine. Made with advanced space-age technology, it had a function not applicable to anything we use here on earth.

But the most intriguing thing of all was the little mongrel with curly brown fur that paced the floor behind the teller. When the dog threw back its head and opened its mouth, I expected the usual sharp "arf, arf" to come out. Instead, he sang out the most beautiful bark I've ever heard. It sounded musical, like a wind instrument. I've never heard anything quite like it before.

Going Forward

The dream world is a fascinating place. As you explore the variety of experiences in the other worlds, you are expanding in your spiritual awareness. Your attitudes change. Awake, you handle certain situations differently than before. You become more diplomatic, more mature, and more responsible. These changes emerge from the experience you are gaining on the inner planes, first in the dream state and later through other methods of inner travel.

At first the dreamer in ECK may not be aware of what is occurring in these other worlds; nevertheless, a change is taking place within him, usually for the better. It is noticeable to his friends, neighbors, and loved ones.

This is not to say that one won't backslide occasionally. Most people go forward for a while, then backward. But at some point, you pick up the pieces and start all over again, keeping your eye on the Sound and Light and on the Mahanta.

The Dream Journal

Though I often recommend keeping a dream journal, I realize it is unrealistic to expect every ECKist to jump up in the middle of every single night to record their dreams. It can become drudgery.

But there is a way to make your dream study a little easier. If you can't do it every night, you can pick one day of the week—Friday is very good—when you make a special effort to write down your dreams.

I have always kept a journal of my inner experiences, but it's impossible to write everything down. Eventually I got into the habit of recording only those experiences that gave me a special insight, even if it would be meaningless to anyone else.

Dry Spells

Sometimes you may go through a dry spell. You are not having the spiritual experiences you would like. There are times of fertile spiritual awareness and other times that feel like a drought—nothing happens. You suspect it never will again. But these ups and downs are all part of living.

Keep in mind that, whether in dreams or in the spiritual exercises, sometimes we fail because we try too hard. It takes practice to get the knack of something new, whether it's tennis, swimming, crocheting, working in the dream state, or anything else that requires skill.

An Exercise to Focus Love

A very good spiritual exercise was given by a RESA (Regional ECK Spiritual Aide) to the ECKists in his area. You can use this technique in place of or preceding your regular spiritual exercise.

There are three steps. Each step is preceded by chanting HU three times.

First you chant HU three times, and then make this statement three times: "I love the SUGMAD, the ECK, and the Mahanta." It centers on love of the three. You are referring, of course, to God, the Holy Spirit, and the Inner Master.

The next step is to chant HU three times, and then say three times: "My consciousness is open to the Sound and Light."

Finally, chant HU three times, then say three times: "I am becoming more aware of the Mahanta."

You can see that there is a progression here. It starts at the top, with love of the SUGMAD, the ECK, and the Mahanta. The next level expresses that your consciousness is open to the Sound and Light, which are the two aspects of the ECK and the Mahanta. The last step, then, is to bring the Mahanta into your conscious awareness.

I think this will help you with your spiritual exercises. It has worked for others.

ECK Creative Arts Festival, Washington, D.C.,
Saturday, June 18, 1988

Within a short time, she had enrolled in acting school. She had made a change in her life that now allows her to do something she finds more fulfilling.

12

The Eternal Dreamer, Part 2

One of the ECKists who performed in the play *Show Time* works in a field not connected to the creative arts. She was fairly content with her job until the day a friend pointed out how unexciting it sounded.

What Would You Like to Do?

"What would you *really* like to do?" the friend prodded.

"I would like to act," the ECKist said, surprising herself. She had never even thought about it before.

Within a short time, she had enrolled in acting school. She had made a change in her life that now allows her to do something she finds more fulfilling.

The opportunities given in ECK often provide a way for a person to break out of an unsatisfying pattern in his or her life. It is not always easy to make a change. But it may be worth it in the long run if you can look back and say, "My life is happier because of it."

Tangible Rewards

A woman was doing volunteer projects for ECK which involved a lot of time. When she began these projects over a year before, she had been several thousand dollars in debt to the credit card companies. Then she got so busy with ECK work that she didn't have time to worry about it.

Just before this ECK seminar, she decided to take an inventory of her finances. She wanted to see how things were going. To her surprise, she was just about out of debt. She hadn't even realized it was happening. She had been so involved in doing something she loved for ECK that she no longer had time to go shopping.

A Sense of Community

I read an article that speculated on why people watch so much television. I suspect it's the same reason they spend so much time shopping. It is a way to recapture the sense of community that has been lost in today's society.

Just a generation or two ago, it was very common for the extended family to live under one roof. If Grandpa and Grandma didn't live with their children and grand-children, they often lived right down the road.

This is less likely today for many reasons. Ours is no longer a predominantly agricultural society: People have moved to the cities. This has given rise to a variety of different life-styles. Plus, the higher cost of living makes a smaller home more feasible. As a result, fewer people live with an extended family.

So people watch television to get a sense of community, to feel they belong to something. We watch TV and shop ourselves into debt because these things tie us to this world and make us feel more a part of it.

Filling Loneliness

This behavior shows a loneliness in people. They are trying to fill it with something. The love, divine or otherwise, simply isn't there.

In ECK we try to open up the inner channel. We look for creative pursuits so that this vacuum within us is filled. We can still watch TV, but we don't have to rely on it. We don't want to be so controlled by our habits that we can't have a life apart from them.

Types of Dreams

Last night I discussed daydreams, initiation dreams, and dreams of intrusion. Today I would like to continue with the other categories of dreams I outlined: release from fear; waking dreams; the Golden-tongued Wisdom; dreams of understanding; and dreams with the Mahanta, which include Light and Sound.

Release from Fear

Many of the habits and karmic patterns that we acquired before coming to ECKANKAR are carried with us as we step onto the path of ECK. These patterns can be limiting. They can even prevent us from rising in consciousness toward the spiritual freedom which is the birthright of Soul.

These limitations often stem from the fears instilled by the religion we followed in the past. They can also be caused by people from our former church attempting to pull us back to the old ways which no longer suit us.

Leaving the Church

One woman came from a strong fundamentalist Christian background, but her religion had never addressed her spiritual questions. The God she had been taught about didn't fit her spiritual needs or expectations. Did that mean there was no God, or just that she would never know for sure? For several years she wavered between being an atheist and an agnostic.

After she joined ECKANKAR, she had a dream where she found herself in an unusual church with her parents. The pulpit stood at floor level, and the pews were elevated on risers that ascended to the back of the church. There were very few people in attendance.

The atmosphere of the church was so heavy and oppressive that the woman became drowsy. She decided to stretch out on the pew to rest. When her parents objected to this display of disrespect for their church, she sat up and made an effort to keep her eyes open. But soon she grew sleepy again, and before long she was lying down.

Suddenly crowds of people poured through the doors. She had to sit up to make room for them. As the service began, she felt very uncomfortable. Why am I here? she wondered. I feel so out of place.

The minister's voice droned on in a dreary sermon. After he finished, the congregation rose and began to sing a song. It was as depressing as the sermon. Oh, no, the woman thought. It was a communion hymn. She did not want to take communion with the others.

Then her attention was drawn to the high, tremulous voice of a female singer several rows behind her. She turned around to look. Just to the left of the singer was the Mahanta, wearing a dark blue suit. Though he was standing up with the rest of the congregation, he was not singing. The Master looked at the dreamer, then smiled and winked.

At that moment the woman knew that the church and all its doctrines no longer had any hold on her. She felt very happy as she turned back to the altar. She was ready now to go up there, just so her parents would not be displeased.

As quickly as she had that thought, the singing stopped and the congregation broke up. Everyone headed for the door. The minister got very upset that the people were leaving his church right in the middle of communion. First he threatened them, then begged, then tried to bribe them into coming back. But they all left anyway.

The woman awoke in the morning with a new outlook. She realized that her fears about the church and Christianity had been taken away. At the same time, she was able to recognize the role her early religion had played in her life, and how it had brought her to ECK.

Your Religious Heritage

It's too easy to say that the religion of our past is old, dead, and no good. It may not be good for us now, but that doesn't mean it can't be beneficial to other people. In a sense, our earlier religion was a good step because it led us to ECK. To deny its place in our life makes no more sense than to cut out any other part of our history.

Unfortunately, that's what some people try to do. With a limited point of view, they would disown their religious heritage because it's not ECK. They think anybody who says that the Christian church has a place in the scheme of things is a heretic in ECK. This is sad. It is the same narrow-mindedness that was and is displayed by some people in fundamentalist religions.

Narrowness of mind is not confined to Christianity, nor is it confined to ECKANKAR. It characterizes a certain state of human consciousness, one that I try to keep away from.

A Break with the Past

For about a year after I came into ECKANKAR, I remained a member of our local country church. Many factors told me that it wasn't time to leave. I was still living at home, helping the family. To be part of the community meant that you went to church.

It also meant that every Sunday I had to walk down the aisle to the communion rail. The ritual had no meaning for me at all, but I recognized that it did for the other members of the church.

One Sunday morning after the service, I finally broke the news to my parents. "I'm not taking communion any more," I told them. Even though I was a grown man, this decision caused quite a disruption at home. Mother threw her hands in the air and carried on as if it were the greatest disaster of all time. Not only had her son quit the ministry to take his chances at the gates of perdition, now he had gone all the way.

She was a good mother who took care of us and loved us very much, but this was the way she saw it. Today, with television and other forms of communication, people are a little more open than they were years ago. They are more willing to accept that there are other ways to think and believe.

God Is More Friendly Now

Many people may not make the connection, but these new channels of communication have changed their concept of God. As they became more receptive to the ideas of others, the laws of God relaxed a little bit too. The God of the old days has become friendlier, more lenient. Just as the God of the Old Testament was replaced by the God of the New Testament, today we find God evolving into an even more expansive being.

The reason for this change is that the consciousness of the people is expanding. Even as recently as thirty years ago, a woman who had a child out of wedlock was treated very shabbily. In the church of my youth, the elders would call the woman before the congregation to answer for her sins. The man was never called forward, of course.

Nowadays when it happens, the same people are more likely to make some concessions. "At least she didn't kill the baby," they'll say.

With the introduction of this new element—abortion— the whole issue of unwed motherhood has changed. The God of thirty or forty years ago was just and righteous and angry at the woman. Today he is pleased that at least she didn't kill the baby. Even against their will, the consciousness of many people has expanded and their God has become more friendly.

Of course, to certain people you wouldn't dare make such a claim. They would be very angry if you implied that attitudes have changed in their religion since they were children. They would defend their childhood God so hotly that you'd have to pull your hat down over your ears and run out of the room.

Waking Dream or Golden-tongued Wisdom?

The waking dream and the Golden-tongued Wisdom are two different categories of experience. Sometimes it is hard to tell which is which.

The waking dream is usually an outer experience given by the Mahanta. Its purpose is to point to a spiritual lesson through an example in your outer life.

The Golden-tongued Wisdom is the voice of the Mahanta that jumps out to impart spiritual insight. It might come through words spoken by another person in a golden moment. The Golden-tongued Wisdom occurs mostly on the outer, but it may also come on the inner planes. The spiritual life includes both our outer and inner lives.

The waking dream usually involves some kind of action in the outer world, and the Golden-tongued Wisdom normally involves voice. That's the only difference, really. Both categories of experience occur in the life of the eternal dreamer.

The Waking Dream

The spiritual life is much broader than just the dream state. Since you do not always remember your experiences on the inner planes, you may feel that you are not making any spiritual progress—but that's not true.

After sixteen years in ECK, a man was feeling frustrated that he'd had so few spiritual experiences. He had written to me about several of them over the years, but somewhere along the way, he forgot them. This is why I recommend keeping a dream journal. These experiences slip away so quickly; if you don't write them down, they are soon forgotten.

One day the ECKist was in his basement listening to a tape of *The Spiritual Notebook* by Paul Twitchell. In chapter 6, Paul discusses the different levels of prayer. Beyond meditation, he says, is a higher form of prayer. This is to place the attention on the crown chakra at the top of the head, and hold it there in contemplation of a lofty truth.

Throughout his years in ECK, the man had been putting his attention at the Tisra Til, the Spiritual Eye. This is located at a point slightly above the center of the eyebrows and about three or four inches back into the head. He now wondered if he should try the crown chakra.

Water on the Ceiling

His wife came downstairs. "There's water running down the wall in the bathroom," she said. So the ECKist went upstairs to look. He traced the leak to the ceiling ventilator. The water was coming in where the caulking had dried out. He could even see daylight through the crack.

Suddenly he saw a connection between the physical imagery and the ideas he had just heard on the tape. The ceiling ventilator is like the crown chakra, he thought. The water coming in is the ECK, or Holy Spirit. Its location in the bathroom probably symbolizes cleansing or purification. The daylight streaming through the crack in the ventilator is the Light of ECK entering through the crown chakra.

The man realized that the water on the ceiling was an outer action from the Mahanta to give him spiritual direction. The ECK was telling him to pay more attention to his spiritual life, to the Light. Above all he was to put attention on the crown chakra. This was a waking dream.

A Lesson with Contact Lenses

A woman who had worn glasses since the age of eight suddenly began to lose her eyesight. The decline took place over a period of three months. Then her right eye started to ache. She tried switching back and forth between her glasses and contacts, but her vision continued to worsen.

"I'm losing my eyesight," she told the optometrist.

"No, you're not," he assured her. "The only thing wrong is that your contact lenses are worn out. After we replace the contacts, your eyes will start to heal. The pain will go away, and your vision will return to normal."

He was right. But the experience had caused her enough worry to catch her attention. She had a feeling there was a deeper meaning behind it. During contemplation she had a conversation with the Mahanta, the Inner Master, on the inner planes.

"What was going on in your life when your eyes began to give you trouble?" he asked.

"I was having a number of difficulties," she said. "Things were not going very well."

"When these difficulties arose, did you have a hard time letting go of something?" he asked.

"No, I don't think so." But as she thought it over, she realized that she had been attached to the way certain things used to be. The more she resisted the changes, the uglier life looked to her. Because her physical eyes now saw life as ugly, her Spiritual Eye began to close. And as the inner vision shut down, her physical eyesight started to fail. It went hand in hand.

The Inner Master tried to get the message to her through her optometrist, who said, "Your contacts are worn out." In other words, your old way of looking at life is wrong; it's worn out. By replacing her contacts, or releasing her attachments to the things that had changed during those three months, she would be able to see clearly again. Spiritually, she could get back on the right track.

The Mahanta used an outer action to give a spiritual lesson—a waking dream.

Wall Hangings

An ECK initiate was trying to make wall hangings for a home. When he ran short of money for supplies, he had to improvise. First, he constructed a wooden frame. Then he stretched the wall hanging over his handiwork, using temporary tacks to hold it in place until he could do it right.

Later he went back to replace the temporary tacks with sturdy, industrial-grade tacks. This would secure the wall hanging to the frame permanently.

He removed the first tack and, poking blindly through the burlap, stuck the permanent one in place. Somehow he managed to hit the same hole that the old tack had been in. That's unusual, he thought. How often can you do that?

He removed another tack, reached for a permanent one, and again, he hit the exact same spot where the old tack had been. The odds of this happening twice were so astronomical that it gave him pause. He began to wonder, Is this a waking dream? If so, what does it mean?

Since the ECK arranges the waking dream to give the individual a spiritual insight, there is a way for him to find the answer for himself.

The ECKist began to look over the situation: Is the waking dream trying to tell me that I'm doing things wrong or right? If I'm doing them wrong, does it mean I'm in a rut? Am I putting my new efforts into the same old pattern?

On the other hand, he thought, could it be that I'm doing things right? Does hitting the same holes twice mean I'm right on target?

Suddenly he knew that this was the case. The feeling of rightness that came with the experience told him that he was right on target. Through an outer action, the Mahanta had given him the spiritual insight to know that he was moving in the correct direction on the path to God. It was not a dramatic experience. But even the little events in life can have an important meaning.

The Golden-tongued Wisdom

The Golden-tongued Wisdom is the voice of the Mahanta that comes through the words of another person. It is usually an outer experience. But as you go further along the path of ECK, you find that the outer world is sometimes hard to differentiate from, say, the Astral world.

These worlds are all a part of you. The first heaven, the Astral world, has as much reality for you as anything that goes on out here. Therefore, the Golden-tongued Wisdom may also come on the inner planes.

Glass Etchings

In the dream state, the Mahanta, the Inner Master, led an ECK initiate down the street to a store with a large glass window. The Mahanta then began to engrave scenes and images on the glass, one after another. The dreamer watched in silence.

"It is best to use images in telling stories," the Mahanta explained as he worked. "The person who is hearing the story can see through the image, just as you can see through the pane of glass. By seeing through the image, the person is able to find the spiritual truth or principle demonstrated by that image."

This was the voice of the Master on the inner planes. The spoken words, along with the images of a mocked-up scene, were used to get a point across to the ECK chela.

Prophecy for the Moment

The Golden-tongued Wisdom comes in many other ways. For example: Something is weighing heavily on your mind, and you are wondering what to do about it. All at once a voice pops out at you from the radio or TV, as if

206

someone just turned up the volume. The words or the phrase may seem completely out of context with what the speaker was saying before. But for you they have a spiritual context that tells you exactly what to do.

The words may carry a simple message from the Master that tells you, "Persevere; continue in what you are doing. You will see the reason for this problem in a very short time. Your spiritual unfoldment will benefit from it."

Or you may be walking down a crowded street, minding your own business. All of a sudden a person nearby speaks a few words to someone else in what seems an abnormally loud voice. The rest of the conversation is a mumble, but what he said at that moment was clear enough to stand out.

This is what I call the Golden-tongued Wisdom. It is part of the ECK-Vidya, the ancient science of prophecy. Its purpose is to give a prophecy for the moment, or an insight into a personal situation.

Dreams of Understanding

An ECKist had a dream where she and another person were in a dimly lit room. There were glass doors covered with heavy, lined drapery that reached from the ceiling to the floor and kept the room in almost total darkness.

The dreamer went up to the drapes and grasped the cord at the side, drawing the drapes open to let more light into the room. Behind the heavy drapery was another curtain; this one was thinner and more sheer. She found the cord for the second set of drapes and pulled on it. As the curtain opened and more light came in, she was able to see just a little better than before. But now she noticed that there were several more layers of drapery behind this one.

"This is crazy," she said. "I don't want to go through all this trouble to pull back the rest of the drapes that are between me and the light. I did the heavy one and the sheer one, but that's enough."

She was very upset when she awoke and remembered the dream. She thought, I had a chance to see the Light of ECK come through clearly in Its pure form, but I didn't open all the drapes.

At this point she remembered a talk I had given during a recent ECK seminar. It was about the many veils that stand between the human consciousness and the higher states of spiritual awareness. We have to be in a higher state of consciousness to see the pure, clear forms of Light or to hear the greater Sound of God.

At our present level, we can handle a certain amount of the Light and Sound, but before we can take in more, we have to reach a higher state of consciousness. To take in more than we are ready for could be harmful. In ECK this is never allowed.

The woman didn't realize that the person with her in the dream was a representative of the Mahanta. She would not have allowed the ECKist to open any more layers of the sheer draperies.

After thinking it over, she understood why she had refused to open all the drapes. Instinctively she had recognized that she could not take all the pure Light that would have come through. She could accept just so much Light and no more. This was a dream of understanding, which can also be called a dream of realization.

A Beached Whale

Another dreamer found himself arriving at a seminar on the inner planes. He entered the dream hotel, walked all the way through to the back, and opened the door. The ocean was so close that water lapped at the edge of the hotel rug. From the doorway he could see whales as they swam back and forth in the bay. Everything was so pretty.

Then he noticed that a small whale was lying on the sand. It had no way to get itself back into the deep water.

One of the bigger whales swam in close and managed to nudge the little one back into the water. Together they rejoined their companions, and they all swam away.

The dreamer understood that he was like the small beached whale, out of his natural element. The big whale symbolized the Mahanta, who had come along to push him back in the water. He was now back in the spiritual waters of life.

A dream like this shows the individual that he is making progress spiritually, and that there is protection and help. This is very important, because sometimes one can feel he is alone in a desert. A dream of water, especially the ocean, represents the fullness or the fulfillment of life. It was reassuring to the dreamer to see a greater creature helping one who was not yet able to fend for himself.

Golden Seeds

An ECKist dreamed that he saw a large sack hanging on a beautiful, ancient tree. The sack was filled with water and golden seeds. A perfectly formed hole in the sack began to open, allowing the water to flow out. But the seeds held back, not wanting to be first. They were afraid of what might happen if they went through the hole with the water. Finally many went, but many stayed.

The golden seeds that went out through the opening with the water were bold and adventuresome. They had no criticism or reproach for the others. Accepting life openly, they went into the ground and were watered and nourished by Spirit. They flourished and bore fruit in another season. They trusted the ECK and prospered. But those who stayed behind withered and died.

This was a highly spiritual dream. What flowed from the sack was the water of life. The seeds were Souls — those who were willing to go with the flow of ECK and those who were not.

The seeds that stayed were fearful of what they might lose if they allowed the water of life to carry them through the opening to another world. And so they held back. But those who went forward found they were now free of the small, old world that once enclosed them. They entered the soil of a grand, new world, where the water allowed the seeds to blossom and grow. Again, this was a spiritual dream of understanding.

Dreams with the Mahanta

The ECK, or Holy Spirit, can be known through Light and Sound. An inner experience with either of these two aspects is actually the presence of the Mahanta, in visible or audible form. When the Light and Sound combine, they form into a single matrix which shows up on the inner planes as the Mahanta, the Inner Master.

An ECK chela had often met the Mahanta on the inner planes but avoided him out of shyness and fear. One night in the dream state she attended a HU Chant in a large hall. Chairs were being set up in several areas, and the people were able to sit where they chose.

The woman selected a certain area and headed in that direction. When she got there, she found the chairs arranged in very disorderly fashion. People were scattered about, sitting here and there; everything was in chaos.

The HU Chant wasn't ready to begin yet, so she decided to leave the hall for a few minutes. As she started to cross the street, she met a few of her friends. They all got into a gondola, the kind used to transport skiers up a slope.

She felt the sensation of being lifted from the ground, and soon the vehicle was gone. In fact, everything was gone. She continued to move very high, very fast, but now there was a noticeable increase in vibration.

This vibration was the Sound of ECK uplifting this person. What started as a dream had turned into a direct experience with the Sound, which showed Itself as vibration.

A few minutes later she found herself back in the body on the plane where the dream had begun. She returned to the hall in time for the HU Chant, but this time she went to an area where the chairs were arranged in an orderly circle. All the seats were taken except for one, and she knew it was hers. She sat down, and the HU Chant began.

Inner Marriage

In the circle was the Mahanta, the Inner Master; but because of her old fears of unworthiness, she kept her eyes down. Then something made her glance up. Looking his way, she suddenly had a feeling of recognition: She had known the Master before, in many lifetimes. She even recollected that he had once printed her wedding invitations.

Rather than an outer marriage, she knew the invitations had been for Soul to be linked up with the ECK. The image actually symbolized an inner marriage between Soul and the Holy Spirit.

For the first time in her experiences on the inner planes, she looked directly into the Master's eyes, and the

211

fear went away. She had reached the degree of unfoldment that allowed her to surrender to the divine principle which operated within her at all times.

Sound Experience

Another dream found two ECK initiates being escorted by the Inner Master through a Temple of Golden Wisdom on the inner planes. As they walked along, suddenly they heard the chanting of HU, sung like a Gregorian chant. The sound went on and on, filling all space.

The two initiates met several other people in the temple, but none were able to hear the sound of HU. To the ECKists it seemed deafening enough to drown out all outer noises. Yet, when the other people spoke, the ECKists could hear them just fine, even over the loud chanting of HU.

This was a direct experience with one of the sounds of God. To hear a number of ECK Masters chanting HU on the inner planes is one of the higher experiences an individual can have in the dream state.

These categories of dreams are by no means complete, but what was given here should provide some guidelines for your experience in the dream state. More will be given in the future.

In the God Worlds of ECK, I am always with you. May the blessings be.

ECK Creative Arts Festival, Washington, D.C.,
Sunday, June 19, 1988

First you have to find out where you are spiritually. You have to know where you are before you can figure out where to go.

13

The Dream of Life

All life is a dream. It is a dream of Soul, a continuation of the dream of SUGMAD. It is a dream of creation and the created; it's a dream of you, your life, and your living of this life.

During this life, you and I have done many things right and many other things that have taught us lessons. We would rather not say we did them wrong, of course. Other people do things wrong; we just had some misfortunes. And they were probably caused by someone else anyway.

By-products of Awareness

Things move very rapidly once an individual comes into ECKANKAR. Sometimes it seems as if the Law of Karma speeds up. But rather than a speeding up of karma, the experience is more a by-product of expanded awareness.

We notice more quickly that our own thoughtlessness comes back to us. In other words, our recognition of paying our karmic debts that we created for ourself comes faster than it used to.

Before we came into ECK, we rarely noticed the times we tripped someone else on the path to God. We did it in the same way as the person who slips into a parking space without even noticing that someone else was just about to pull into it. He has no idea that the other guy was there first and was greatly inconvenienced by the thoughtless act.

The dream of life starts out here in our everyday life. As we go about our daily activities, trying to make life happy and fun, occasionally we put our foot in our mouth. We hurt another person's feelings. If we happen to recognize it, we try to make it right, but often end up making it worse. If we have any grace at all, we just excuse ourself from the scene and hope that the lesson is over and forgotten by all. Usually it is not.

Chris's Red Ball

One morning an ECKist was working in his backyard while his daughters played nearby. A small boy named Chris was happily kicking a red ball back and forth in the next yard. When he accidentally kicked it into the ECKist's yard, Chris ran over to get it.

The little boy couldn't speak very well yet. "I want my wed ball," he said.

"Oh, you want the wed ball?" the man said, mimicking Chris. The little guy was at an age where he couldn't talk any better, but he knew he was being mocked, and he was very embarrassed. The other kids picked up on it and began to make fun of him.

The man saw what was happening and tried to make things better. "Uh, wed ball is OK," he said. "I do tongue twisters myself all the time." His comment struck the other kids as hilarious. Now they really went crazy in making fun of little Chris. The man had only made a bad situation worse.

216

Poor little guy, he thought. I wish I hadn't done that to him, but I don't know how to get him out of this fix. Maybe I'd better just go in the house.

Later that day the ECKist went for a walk with his dog. Along the way he met a stranger, an individual as talkative as the man was, and soon they were engaged in conversation. But no matter what subject they discussed, the ECKist's tongue kept tripping over itself. He couldn't utter one coherent sentence. The words came out as if his tongue were glued to the top of his mouth. Every time he spoke, the stranger gave him a confused look. The man was so embarrassed that his face turned the color of Chris's little red ball.

Suddenly he made the connection between his inability to talk properly and his unintentional mocking of the little boy. He realized that a situation he'd created for someone else had come right back to him.

The karma did come back to him rather quickly. For many people it takes longer. By the time it gets back to them, they have forgotten what they did to bring it on. This is especially true of those who have no understanding of the Law of Action and Reaction.

For the ECKist, what started out as a lighthearted dream of life slowly turned into a nightmare before the day was over. But the presence of the Inner Master is always with the ECK initiate, arranging ways to give him spiritual insight. It was no accident that the man's tongue got twisted at a time when he could learn something from the experience.

The Tow Truck

An ECK initiate lives in Trinidad, West Indies. Late one night his son called to say he had been in an accident.

217

The car was so badly damaged that it wasn't drivable. "It's in the middle of the intersection, blocking traffic," his son said.

As soon as the father arrived at the scene of the accident, the police told him, "You must move this car out of here right now." Most of us would simply call a twenty-four-hour towing service to take the car away. But in Trinidad businesses are usually closed by 10:00 p.m. It was now 11:30 p.m.

"Where am I going to find a tow truck at this hour?" the father asked the policemen. "We don't care where," they said. "Just get that car out of here."

The man walked to a phone booth and began thumbing through the yellow pages. He called several service stations, but none answered at that late hour. He didn't know what to do. Finally he said, "Mahanta, I can't find a tow truck anywhere, and the police are threatening to fine me if I don't get my son's car out of the intersection. Please help me."

From out of the dark came a loud chugging sound. The ECKist looked up and saw that it was a tow truck. He quickly left the phone booth, flagged the truck down, and explained his predicament. The two men in the truck were more than willing to help. They agreed to move the car and put it in storage for the weekend, at a very reasonable cost.

The ECKist was curious. Just as the truck was about to pull away, he asked the men, "Why were you driving by here so late? Were you on your way home? Is this the route you normally take?"

"Actually, we have never come this way before," the driver said. "We just happened to be in the neighborhood and decided to take this street."

The driver's answer merely confirmed what the ECKist already knew: In his time of trouble, the Mahanta was there to help.

Calling On the Master

Practicing the presence of the Master is an ECK principle that is often forgotten. In times of trouble, some people find it easier to remember the cusswords they learned before coming to ECK—usually those tried-and-true words that take God's name in vain. After all, they figure, why experiment with something different at a critical time like this? The profanities may not help, but at least they're familiar.

It is quite a discipline to remember to call upon the Inner Master and say, "Mahanta, I need help. If there is some way that an individual Soul in the great collection of Souls that live in this world can help, please send that Soul."

Once you become an ECKist, you begin to learn to ask for help. Eventually it becomes second nature. Further along in ECK you find that you don't specifically have to ask; it is enough to simply recognize that the Master is always with you, and to live with that reality all the time. You look for a way out of the problem, knowing that the ECK, the Holy Spirit, will bring the help when it is needed. But it will come in a way that also teaches you something about yourself spiritually.

If you are an individual who does not like to ask for help, you may be placed in a position where you have to ask for help. The purpose is to strengthen you where you are weakest. This is how the Master works.

The Fateful Bus Trip

One level of the dream of life is the waking dream, which involves an experience in our outer life. It could happen just as easily in the dream state, where the meaning might be as clear as a bell. But because it takes place in the course of our daily life, we tend to overlook the spiritual significance. We are so involved in the experience that we can't step back and see what the Master is trying to show us.

An initiate from Canada wanted to go to an ECK seminar in Washington, D.C., but found herself short of money. When other ECKists in her area hired a bus to take them to the seminar, she decided to join them. She really preferred to fly, but the bus was much more affordable. Besides, with the air conditioning, it would be a comfortable ride.

The woman didn't get a wink of sleep the night before they were to leave. Since the trip would take twelve hours, she looked forward to sleeping as they traveled. But as soon as the bus left Montreal, a series of problems began.

First the air conditioning stopped working, and then the toilet backed up. The bus grew uncomfortably warm and the air turned foul, but the woman was so tired that she tried to rest anyway. Just as she was on the verge of sleep, the other ECKists decided it would be fun to sing all the way to Washington.

To top it off, the bus driver took a wrong turn and got lost. Unfamiliar with the route, he ended up exploring mile after mile of scenic side roads that nobody cared to see. The trip took sixteen hours. By the time the woman stumbled off the bus, she was very upset.

She wanted to enjoy the seminar, but she had a hard time keeping her attention on the speakers or participating in the workshops. She kept thinking about that horrible bus ride. It was the most awful trip she had ever experienced in her life—and to an ECK seminar of all places! She couldn't stop stewing.

That evening she was standing in the hall, waiting to

get into the main session, when one of her friends from Canada tapped her on the shoulder. She immediately blurted out all the ordeals she had suffered on the bus trip—"no sleep, the toilet backed up, the air conditioning broke, the trip took four extra hours from getting lost, and everybody sang like hyenas!"

The other ECKist listened patiently to her sad tale. When she finally wound down, he said, "What an interesting dream!"

The woman almost had a fit. "I don't believe you understood me," she snapped. "I didn't say this was a dream. It was my bus trip from Montreal to this seminar!"

"But think about it," the other initiate said. "At this seminar, the attention is on dreams."

The woman stared at him for a minute, and then her anger faded. "Why, of course," she said. "It was a waking dream." Suddenly she saw the spiritual story behind that fateful bus trip and knew that the Master had given her the experience to teach her something about herself.

The bus symbolized herself as Soul, and the trip was a parallel of Soul making Its journey home to God. She compared the broken air conditioning to what happened when she lost her patience and got hot under the collar. The backed-up toilet represented the problems she experienced when she ate the wrong foods. The constant noise on the bus reminded her of the times she talked when she should have listened.

The woman now saw the entire bus trip as a journey to a greater spiritual understanding of herself. She knew that the inner teachings had been given to her even before she arrived at the seminar. With this realization, the cloud that had hung over her seminar experience went away, and she was able to enjoy the rest of the weekend.

221

End of the World?

Occasionally people have a dream that tells them the end of the world is coming. Individuals not familiar with the ECK teachings have been known to take the dream literally. A few have even gone to a printer and spent their last dime on posters and brochures that proclaim, "The End of the World Is Coming!" With doomsday so near, what else do they need the money for?

A woman had a dream like this, but fortunately she was in ECK. Though she didn't understand what it meant at first, she knew that the Inner Master was trying to teach her something.

In the dream she was listening to the news. Suddenly a scientist interrupted the newscaster to announce that the world was coming to an end. "The sun is moving closer to earth," he explained. "Four days from now it's going to explode, and everything in the world will be burned to a crisp. The sun will then begin to cool down, but the earth will be no more than a cold lump of matter, floating aimlessly through space."

"I've got four days left," she said to herself. "How do I want to spend them?" Being a sensible woman, she decided to take off from work.

"The scientists predict it's going to be like a huge nuclear explosion," she told her husband. "If there's no way to avoid the destruction, I might as well enjoy these last few days. And when the explosion comes, I'm going to watch it for as long as I remain in this physical body."

On the last day, she and her husband stayed in their home. Through the window they watched the sun grow larger and redder. "Oh, what a beautiful sight!" they said.

Just then the first explosion came, knocking out all the windows. They ducked and tried to avoid the flying glass, but the woman got a cut on her knee. "Let me get you a Band-Aid," her husband offered.

"Don't be silly," she said. "Let's just watch this while we can." Just as her lifetime on the other plane came to an end, she awoke from the dream.

Strengthen Your Weak Points

The dream stayed with her for quite a while. She was pleased to notice that she hadn't reacted to it with fear, as she might have done before coming into ECK. Still, she tried to interpret it in terms of her daily life. Was it a warning that something catastrophic was going to happen in four days? A family crisis? Her health?

Driving in her car later that week, she thought about all her problems. She began a mental conversation with the Inner Master about the many things that were bothering her. "Mahanta, can you please take these troubles away from me?" she asked.

The answer she got from the Master was very interesting: "You just had an experience in a dream of losing everything, even your own life. Nothing in this present life should ever trouble you again."

The answer gave her a new perspective on her troubles; they didn't seem so big anymore. She realized that this dream of apparent catastrophe was actually meant to strengthen her in her daily life.

What's the Purpose?

The experiences that you have in ECK—including dreams, Soul Travel, the ECK-Vidya, and seeing the Light or hearing the Sound of God—are not about the past or the future. Their purpose is to give you another perspective on your life today.

People occasionally have a dream about a past life with another person. Misunderstanding its purpose, they may use it to try to put a hold on that person, who has no recollection of the mutual past life. It becomes a control factor.

When the Inner Master shows you a karmic picture from a past life, it is mainly to give you an insight into yourself as you are today—the most perfect spiritual being you have ever been in all your lives. That is who you are today.

By the same token, if the Master gives you an experience about a future event, the aspect about the future is secondary. Again, it is really about today. If you keep this in mind, you will interpret the experience in a way that will give you more perspective about your present life and how you can live it better.

At the Crossroad

The real importance of dream symbology is in how it relates spiritually to your daily life. An ECKist discovered this through a dream about his wife, who is not in ECKANKAR.

In their outer life, his wife appeared somewhat interested in ECK, but she wasn't quite sure that she wanted to become a member. At various times she had also considered either staying in her present religion or looking into some other spiritual teaching. She often discussed her dilemma with her husband.

One night the husband dreamed that his wife called him at home. She said, "I'm at a phone booth, but I don't know where I am. I'm lost. Can you help me get home?"

"If you know the name of the road you're on, or even a nearby crossroad, I can help you find your way home," the husband said.

"There aren't any crossroads around here," she said. "I don't know where I am."

"OK, get in the car and drive down the street very slowly until you come to an intersection. Then call me back and tell me the names of the two crossroads. We'll be able to figure out where you are."

The ECKist woke up wondering what the dream was all about. The experience on the inner planes had been so lifelike that he knew it was trying to tell him something.

Suddenly he realized it was an answer to his fear that he may have been pushing ECKANKAR on his wife. At times he thought she seemed truly interested in the teachings of the Holy Spirit. But he had often wondered, Does she really care, or am I only imagining her interest?

The dream had given him a spiritual understanding of his wife's position. She was in the car, and she was lost. This represents Soul's journey through the lower worlds as It tries to find Its way home. But until she had at least some idea of where she was, her husband couldn't help her.

All he could do in the dream was encourage her to go very slowly down the road until she came to a crossroad. This gave him the insight to tell her out here, "First you have to find out where you are spiritually. You have to know where you are before you can figure out where to go."

He recommended that she examine her own religion, other spiritual paths, ECKANKAR, and whatever else she wanted to, but to go very slowly. Eventually she would come to a point in her life that seemed significant. Then she could stop, take a look around, and see where she was. Her husband could then try to help her figure out her direction home.

How Do I Get Home?

Soul, feeling lost in the lower worlds, often has to ask someone else, "How do I get home?" Helping others in this way is part of the service ECKists can provide without assuming a heavy missionary role.

We try to be there for people who ask, but we don't try to persuade anybody who doesn't care to hear about ECK. If someone is happy on his present spiritual path, that's where he belongs. He should be allowed to stay there in peace.

On the other hand, if someone is unhappy on his spiritual path, including ECKANKAR, then he should look around until he finds the path that will make him happy. Not everybody wants to be a Christian; nor is everyone destined or cut out to be an ECKist. This is as it should be. Each of us is a unique individual.

Going to the Front of the Line

Help received upon asking is another aspect of the dream of life. A man in Africa had to take his son to a medical clinic. The boy had become very ill during the night. When they arrived at the clinic at 9:00 a.m., there was already a long line of people waiting to see the doctor.

At 1:00 p.m. the man began to wonder if his son would ever get in for treatment. People who had lined up at 6:30 a.m. were still ahead of him in the waiting room. The boy was growing sicker by the hour, and the line didn't seem to be moving at all.

The ECKists in Africa have to be many times stronger in ECK than the initiates in the more developed countries. Not only is life in general often more difficult, but in certain countries their lives and freedom are threatened just for being followers of ECK.

226

The man remembered a spiritual technique he had read about in an ECK publication. It was simply this: Visualize yourself where you are right now, then chant HU, the sacred name of God, and imagine yourself where you want to be.

The man began to chant HU. He visualized himself and his son walking to the very front of the long line. Then he imagined them going through the door to the examining room, where a doctor stood ready to treat his son.

After he had done the spiritual exercise for a few minutes, one of the doctors came into the waiting room from outside. He saw the ECKist's son lying on a sofa, sweating heavily.

"Whose son is this?" the doctor asked.

"He is my son," said the ECKist.

"What's the matter with him?" After the father explained, the doctor said, "We will do the paperwork now and treat him right away. He may be very sick."

A clerk came all the way down the long line to the man and his son, and escorted them to the front of the line. The boy got treated immediately.

It took the man four hours of waiting in line to remember to chant HU. When he did, he recognized how quickly came the help of the Mahanta. The doctor happened to come in just after the man began to chant HU. Whether it was part of his illness or not, the boy just happened to be sweating at a good time to catch the doctor's eye.

Spirit of Love

As much as we hate to admit it, often it takes inconvenience or pain to help us unfold spiritually. But sometimes people ask too quickly to have their troubles taken away. This is because they haven't yet learned the real meaning of the presence of the Mahanta.

The spiritual power is always with you, wherever you are. It's there whenever you are in trouble, and when you are not in trouble. It is the spirit of love, an overwhelming love that gives protection and strength and comfort. It is a love that has the greatest compassion for you as you struggle to understand your life and make your way to the Kingdom of Heaven.

Call This Number Now

An ECKist on the East Coast put a listing in the local ECKANKAR newsletter so people could call a special number at her house for information on local events. She installed a separate phone and hooked up an answering machine to take the calls.

About 11:30 one night, a man called and left an unusual message. He had fallen asleep and had a dream. In it, a man he described as being on the thin side, dressed in a nightshirt, had told him, "Dial one for long distance, then these ten digits." The dreamer didn't realize it, but this was the Inner Master.

The dreamer was startled awake. Without knowing why, he had an urge to call the number right away. It turned out to be the information phone at the ECKist's house in a neighboring state. Since he hadn't left a number, the woman was unable to call him back.

A second call came the next night, about 3:30 a.m. In this message, the caller described himself as a simple farmer in North Carolina. All he was trying to do, he said, was get some sleep, but these strangers kept interrupting, telling him to call the same number.

This time there were two men in the dream. "The man in the nightshirt was with another fellow. He had dark, wavy hair and appeared to be of Mongolian descent," the caller said. This, of course, was the Tibetan ECK Master Rebazar Tarzs.

A few days later he called again, and the ECKist answered the phone. The man had never heard of ECKANKAR, and he wanted to find out what it was all about. The ECKist told him a little about dream travel and Soul Travel. She also talked about the Sound and Light of God, and the word *HU*. The man began to open up to her.

While in the army, he said, he had gotten very ill. He'd had a Code Blue, a near-death experience that had frightened him very much. He had seen his deceased mother and aunt, who now lived on the Astral Plane. "There is a beautiful world here," they said. "We can show it to you if you want to come with us." The choice was his: stay on earth or come to this other world.

Inwardly he decided to stay; outwardly the doctors revived him. But he had been terrified of death ever since. Now, he said, the men in the dream were telling him, "If you want to get over your fear of death, call this number."

On top of that, he was now having out-of-body experiences. "I'm worried that I'm losing my mind," he said, "because I seem to have this separation from the body. I'm not quite sure, but I think I'm going crazy."

"No," said the ECKist. "It's a very normal thing." She explained to him that there were quite a few people in ECKANKAR who had the very same experiences. "Once you get used to it, you won't find it fearful at all. You'll find it joyful to be able to move with such freedom, even while still here in the physical body."

The next time the man called, he said, "I've been Soul traveling to your town." He accurately described the streets and a river nearby. "I find myself in these rooms where people are sitting in small groups, talking about spiritual things. At other times I'm in some sort of temple." He sounded less upset now, as if he was beginning to accept these new developments.

Spiritual Perspective

The woman who answered the phone had not yet had the experience of Soul traveling, and she thought this man was very fortunate. But not every ECKist needs to Soul Travel. Some are here simply to meet people who are having these experiences and need an explanation. When the time is right, one of the ECK Masters on the inner planes will give the person very clear instructions on how to find ECKANKAR.

When this happens, an ECKist doesn't really have to do much more than direct them toward the ECK books, if they even want that. Because from then on, the Inner Master takes over and helps the individual on his own path home to God.

Some of these experiences also happen to people in other religions. If they don't have the spiritual perspective we learn in ECKANKAR, they become fearful and wonder if they're losing their mind. But others are more open to the guidance they are given on the inner planes. They will find their way to an ECKist, who will tell them about the SUGMAD, the ECK, the Mahanta, and the Light and Sound of God.

The End Goal

The spiritual exercise used by the man who was trying to get his son treated by a doctor is helpful when you run into obstacles that prevent you from getting something done.

Chant HU and visualize yourself reaching your goal, whatever you wish to achieve. In the earlier example, the man wished to have his son seen by a doctor. While chanting HU, he imagined himself walking with his son past a long line of people, going into the examining room, and being greeted by the doctor who would treat the boy.

This technique is to be used only for yourself; it is not to be used to push other people out of the way. To control the actions of anyone else is a form of black magic. You can use this technique because you need treatment, you need to get something done, or you need to be here or there. If it is in compliance with all the invisible spiritual laws, it will happen.

As long as you chant HU and do the technique in an open, trusting way, only good can happen. You will never be allowed to intrude upon another person's space, because at this point you are living the spiritual life in a waking dream.

ECK European Seminar, The Hague, The Netherlands, Saturday, July 30, 1988

In the ten minutes the game lasted, I watched him transform from a person who played only for himself to one who was willing to help another.

14

Lessons from the Master

The title of today's talk is "Lessons from the Master." One example of this took place in a video arcade. The arcades provide a good way to be among people. Also, playing video games helps me to work off tension. You might think a person in my position wouldn't have any tension. But the fact is, there is a lot.

Playing Doubles

Occasionally I go to a video arcade in a run-down section of town, patronized mainly by youth from the streets, some of them a bit rowdy. As I was leaving the arcade one day, I walked past a black youth who looked to be about fifteen. "You wanna play doubles on this game?" he said.

Playing doubles usually isn't done among strangers in video parlors, and frankly, it's something I prefer not to do anyway. "No, thanks," I said. "I've played enough today. I'm ready to go home."

"I'll pay," he offered. "I've got a lot of tokens."

I realized the money for his tokens would not be easy to come by. If he wanted to play badly enough to pay for two players, he must really like the game. It showed that he cared about something, and to me that means a lot. "Don't worry about it," I said. "I'll pay for my own game. Let's play."

Your opponents in this particular game are snapping turtles, pests, and fireballs. They try to hurt you. The two players can either attempt to protect each other or they can work against each other, until the game finally gobbles you both up. The game has to end sometime, and eventually you make enough mistakes that the game wins and you lose.

"What kind of a score do you average?" I asked.

"Hundred thousand points," he said.

"I'm lucky to get fifty thousand on this game," I said, "but let's give it a try."

As we started to play, I could tell he had a bit of a chip on his shoulder—teenager versus adult. We were both fighting common opponents, but at first he played only for himself.

At one point I tried my best to help him out of a very tight spot. But I wasn't skilled enough at this particular game, so he lost a player. "Doggone it," I said, "I tried to save you, but I couldn't. I just don't play well enough."

A change came over him when he saw that I was working with him, not against him. He quickly turned his efforts to trying to help me too. Suddenly we were working as a team, fighting off the turtles, pests, and fireballs together. In the ten minutes the game lasted, I watched him transform from a person who played only for himself to one who was willing to help another. We both ended up with very poor scores, but we had a good time getting there.

He didn't know it, but for him this was a lesson from the Master. The experience was to give him a different outlook, and this may affect the way he deals with other people.

God, Stop the Rain

An elderly ECKist was going to a social with a Christian friend. The social was put on for retired people by an insurance company who wanted to sell them insurance, and refreshments were being provided to soften them up for the sales talk.

As the two women got into the car, it began to rain heavily. It was coming down in sheets by the time they arrived at the place where the social was being held. "We forgot our umbrellas," the ECKist's friend said. "We'll be drenched by the time we get inside."

The ECKist said, "Well, God, if we're supposed to go in there without getting soaked, could you please stop the rain?" Lo and behold, the rain stopped.

The two women went inside and enjoyed the social. When they got to the door to leave, it was pouring again; but just as they stepped outside, the rain stopped. They drove home without thinking much about it.

Later in the day, they went grocery shopping together. This time they brought their umbrellas, just in case. Sure enough, by the time they got to the store, it was raining heavily once more. The ECKist reached for her umbrella and started to get out of the car.

"Why not ask God to stop the rain?" the Christian woman said. "It worked last time."

"God knows when I need help or not," the ECKist replied. "God knows I have my umbrella this time."

Without using a whole bunch of strange-sounding ECK terms, the ECKist pointed out a spiritual principle to the other woman. It's the same idea expressed in the story

235

about a traveler who asked the village sage, "Should I pray to God to keep the thieves from stealing my camel, or would I be better off to just tie up the animal?" The sage's reply: "Pray to God, and tie up your camel."

Asking for Divine Help

We ask for divine help when we need it, but not when the situation is within our own power to resolve. Too often we have the feeling that no matter what comes up, there must be an easy way out. Instead of using our God-given creative abilities to figure out a way to overcome the problem, we want someone else to take care of it. We are actually cheating ourselves as spiritual beings.

An ECKist who is operating at his absolute best will ask, What resources has the ECK put at my disposal so that I can solve the problem myself? By doing this, he knows that he is exercising his spiritual muscles.

Power of Love

One of the most important lessons from the Master is that love is stronger than power. An initiate found this out several years ago when a group of Baptists came to picket an ECK seminar. Their motive was to convince the ECKists that Christ was the way to salvation, and their method was to push Bibles and brochures at them as they entered the seminar site.

The initiate was seated on a low, decorative wall outside the hall, watching the goings-on. Some of the ECKists were trying to get the Baptists to leave. "You don't have any right to be here," they insisted forcefully. They had a point, in a way. Would they feel the ECKists had the right to picket a Sunday-morning Baptist service and try to force ECK literature on the congregation? Not only would that be in poor taste, it shows a lack of respect for the freedom of others.

As the ECKist sat quietly on the wall, one of the Baptists, a handsome young man, came up to her and said, "Do you know that Christ has saved you?"

Instead of giving a direct response, the ECKist asked him a question: "What is God?"

The Baptist went right into a lively sermon about salvation through Christ, justification by faith, and what religion meant to him. The ECKist listened politely, without interrupting. When at last he paused for breath, she simply said, "I am June, and I love you."

The young man obviously didn't know quite what to say to this. He tried to resume his talk on salvation but finally changed the subject and began to talk about his family problems.

"My wife and children don't appreciate me," he said, "and I don't know why. I am a dutiful husband, a loving father, and a compassionate human being. Yet for all the good that I do for my family, they don't have any respect for me."

The ECKist listened quietly as the young man unburdened himself of his troubles. When he was finished, he just looked at her for a minute. Finally he said, "I am John, and I love you."

They talked some more, and before he left to rejoin his friends she gave him a copy of *ECKANKAR—The Key to Secret Worlds* plus several ECK brochures. Then he went over to his friends and said, "Come on, time to go." She watched him tuck his Bible under his arm and begin thumbing through the ECK book. He and his friends were still discussing it as they walked away.

The woman had noticed how the power of love could change the direction of a situation. Whereas the other ECKists had tried to force the Baptists to go away, it was love that overcame the intrusion. This was her lesson from the Master.

Buzzing Bees

When an ECKist's father translated, she went to stay with her mother for a while. Soon after the funeral, she got a call from her father's sister. The aunt wanted to know how the ECKist and her mother were getting along, but there was also another reason for her call.

"I'm not psychic," said the aunt, a born-again Christian for twenty-four years, "but something very strange happened to me."

About the time her brother had translated, the woman said, "a sudden feeling of tiredness came over me. I went to my bedroom and lay down to rest. As soon as I closed my eyes, I heard a strange sound, like buzzing bees."

The aunt opened her eyes, and before her was the face of her brother, just as it had looked when he was young and healthy. Yet she knew that during his illness his weight had dwindled to seventy pounds. Her brother's face appeared, then disappeared, three times. Each appearance was accompanied by the sound of buzzing bees.

"What happened?" she asked her niece. "What does it mean?"

"You saw your brother on the other side," the ECKist said. "He has regained his youth, and that's the way he looks now."

Then she explained, "The buzzing of bees is the sound on the plane, or heaven, where he is now living." In ECK we know that the buzzing of bees is the Sound of the Holy Spirit as It is heard on the Etheric Plane.

Encouraging Words

Many people outside of ECK have experiences with the Light and Sound of the Holy Spirit. But usually they do not understand them.

As channels for the ECK, or Holy Spirit, ECKists are able to give encouraging words. We are often placed in a certain position to be of help to someone who is seeking the Light, or has a question about the Light and Sound.

If they are afraid, or think the experience means that there is something wrong with them, we can assure them: "No, you do not need a psychiatrist; you are perfectly sane. What you are having is a spiritual experience from the highest source. It does not fall in the category of psychic phenomena or anything of this nature. The Sound you hear is the Voice of God, the Holy Spirit, which we call the ECK."

What Is Detachment?

Sometimes an individual gets a lesson from the Master on detachment. Detached love is a term that comes up a lot in the ECK teachings. It is not always understood.

In the early years of ECKANKAR, some ECKists equated detachment with coldness. In other words, if someone needed a shoulder to cry on, the ECKist practiced his idea of detached love by standing rigid and strong, like an ivory pillar. But other people couldn't quite relate to this. It was more like leaning against a wooden post than another human being.

Detached love means listening patiently to someone talk, simply because that person has a need to talk. If they need to cry, you can be there to provide a shoulder for them to cry on until they can be healed of whatever is causing their sorrow.

One definition of detachment is to allow other people to have their emotions. Emotions are a very natural part of living. But it also has another meaning.

An ECKist received a special edition of *The Shariyat-Ki-Sugmad,* which came complete with leather cover. She was so proud of this book that she thought about putting it in her home on a pedestal under glass. She knew that some of the ECKists had seen the Shariyat displayed this way in Temples of Golden Wisdom on the inner planes, where the pages glowed with light and turned by themselves.

After admiring her beautiful new book for a while, she set it on her coffee table and went out to a meeting. She came home later to find her dog happily chewing on the cover. In fact, a piece of the cover was still hanging from the dog's mouth.

The woman was beside herself. "Don't you know that books are precious?" she said to the dog. I suspect he did know that they were precious, but in a different way.

As she thought it over, she realized that for the last three weeks she had been giving her dog leather chew-toys to chew on. When he sniffed the leather book cover, naturally he thought it was his. He then helped himself to this very high-grade leather toy.

The following week, the woman attended an ECK Satsang class and mentioned the incident to the Arahata. The Arahata's response is an example of an ECKist's ability to see the larger picture. She said, "But did the dog eat any words?"

"No," the woman said. "As a matter of fact, the dog didn't eat any of the words at all. None of the print on the cover was missing."

After she digested the Arahata's words, she became reconciled to the fact that the dog had digested her book cover. Then she realized that the Master had given her a lesson in detachment. The book had been very precious to her; but how important, really, should we allow any physical object to be?

When word got back to me about what had happened, I asked the staff to send her a new book for herself. "Tell her she is welcome to keep the other book for her dog," I said.

Not for ECKists Only

A Higher Initiate in ECK scheduled a viewing of "The Journey Home" video as part of an introductory presentation on ECKANKAR. She had reserved a motel room for the presentation. Since it was during the motel's busy season, they were booked solid.

Several ECKists arrived early to hook up the VCR. But no matter what they tried, they couldn't get "The Journey Home" to play.

The presentation was scheduled to begin at 8:00 p.m., and they were running out of time. They called for help. A maintenance man came to the room. He began to fiddle with the wires, trying different combinations of hookups between the VCR and the TV. Nothing he did could make the VCR work.

While he was busy with the technical end of the problem, the ECKists began to discuss the spiritual aspects of the situation. The maintenance man no doubt wondered why these people considered their VCR to be a spiritual matter, but he was polite enough not to ask.

Finally he said, "Look, it's almost eight o'clock. The only thing I can think of is to run this film on the movie channel. That means it would be shown throughout the motel. I'm sorry," he said, "that's the only way I can do it."

The ECKists were delighted, of course. At 8:00 p.m., "The Journey Home" was shown in place of the regularly scheduled movie on every TV in the sold-out motel.

As guests checked out the next morning, they had some very good comments about the film, according to the owner of the motel. Some told her how enjoyable it had made their stay. She was so pleased about it that when the Higher Initiate tried to pay for the room, the owner wouldn't take any money.

The situation worked out well for everyone involved. Lessons from the Master are not only for the ECKists.

Expectations

At an ECK seminar recently, I ended a talk without saying, "May the blessings be," as I usually do. One of the initiates was very upset by this. It struck her strongly. Each time she heard that phrase, she felt the warmth and love of God and the Holy Spirit going out to her. She wondered why I had not said it after that particular talk.

Finally it came to her that I had been speaking about expectations—those we have about Divine Spirit and about other people. When our expectations are not met, we feel let down in spirit. Does the fault lie with the people who let us down, or were our expectations too high?

She saw that she had been unrealistic to expect the ECK teachings to always come through outer channels. This included the blessings of the SUGMAD in the phrase "May the blessings be." The true message of ECK is always given on the inner planes, by the Inner Master.

The Keystone of ECK

The message that I give on the outer is just a link. It is a way for you to connect with the teachings on the inner planes, so that one day you can have a stronger linkup with the ECK flow, the love of ECK.

Love is the keystone of ECK: God is love, ECK is love, the Holy Spirit is love, and you are love. This is what you are trying to achieve in your realizations. As you rise to the higher states of consciousness, you become not a greater servant of God, but a greater channel of love to all life for the Divinity which is, in whatever way you see or know IT.

The teachings of ECKANKAR are the teachings of love. And with love comes compassion, understanding, wisdom, and freedom.

May the blessings be.

ECK European Seminar, The Hague, The Netherlands, Sunday, July 31, 1988

Glossary

Words set in SMALL CAPS are defined elsewhere in the glossary.

ARAHATA. An experienced and qualified teacher for ECKANKAR classes.

CHELA. A spiritual student.

ECK. The Life Force, the Holy Spirit, or Audible Life Current which sustains all life.

ECKANKAR. Religion of the Light and Sound of God. Also known as the Ancient Science of SOUL TRAVEL. A truly spiritual religion for the individual in modern times, known as the secret path to God via dreams and SOUL TRAVEL. The teachings provide a framework for anyone to explore their own spiritual experiences. Established by Paul Twitchell, the modern-day founder, in 1965.

ECK MASTERS. Spiritual Masters who can assist and protect people in their spiritual studies and travels. The ECK Masters are from a long line of God-Realized SOULS who know the responsibility that goes with spiritual freedom.

HU. The secret name for God. The singing of the word HU, pronounced like the man's name Hugh, is considered a love song to God. It is sung in the ECK Worship Service.

INITIATION. Earned by the ECK member through spiritual unfoldment and service to God. The initiation is a private ceremony in which the individual is linked to the Sound and Light of God.

LIVING ECK MASTER. The title of the spiritual leader of ECKANKAR. His duty is to lead SOULS back to God. The Living ECK Master can assist spiritual students physically as the Outer Master, in the dream state as the Dream Master, and in the spiritual worlds as the

245

Inner Master. Sri Harold Klemp became the Living ECK Master in 1981.

MAHANTA. A title to describe the highest state of God Consciousness on earth, often embodied in the LIVING ECK MASTER. He is the Living Word.

PLANES. The levels of heaven, such as the Astral, Causal, Mental, Etheric, and Soul planes.

SATSANG. A class in which students of ECK study a monthly lesson from ECKANKAR.

THE SHARIYAT-KI-SUGMAD. The sacred scriptures of ECKANKAR. The scriptures are comprised of twelve volumes in the spiritual worlds. The first two were transcribed from the inner PLANES by Paul Twitchell, modern-day founder of ECKANKAR.

SOUL. The True Self. The inner, most sacred part of each person. Soul exists before birth and lives on after the death of the physical body. As a spark of God, Soul can see, know, and perceive all things. It is the creative center of Its own world.

SOUL TRAVEL. The expansion of consciousness. The ability of SOUL to transcend the physical body and travel into the spiritual worlds of God. Soul Travel is taught only by the LIVING ECK MASTER. It helps people unfold spiritually and can provide proof of the existence of God and life after death.

SOUND AND LIGHT OF ECK. The Holy Spirit. The two aspects through which God appears in the lower worlds. People can experience them by looking and listening within themselves and through SOUL TRAVEL.

SPIRITUAL EXERCISES OF ECK. The daily practice of certain techniques to get us in touch with the Light and Sound of God.

SUGMAD. A sacred name for God. SUGMAD is neither masculine nor feminine; IT is the source of all life.

WAH Z. The spiritual name of Sri Harold Klemp. It means the Secret Doctrine. It is his name in the spiritual worlds.

Index

247

Car, 11–12, 138–39
Cat, 33–35, 48–49, 164–65
    orange, 133–37
Causal Plane. *See* Plane(s):
    Causal
Cave(s), 171–72
Challenge(s), 83, 187
Change(s)
    ECK brings, 110
    life, 19, 126, 128, 140, 195
    Mahanta brings, 112, 234
    resistance to, 204
    when the rules, 59
    Wind of, 125
Channel(s)
    for ECK, 2, 163, 164, 239
    for Holy Spirit, 48, 71, 93
    of love, 243
Chant. *See* HU: Chant; HU:
    chanting
Charity, 140
Child(ren), 44–45, 55–56, 216,
    226–27
Chiropractor, 1–2
Choice, 10, 12, 29
Chris's-red-ball story, 216–17
Christian(ity), 116, 175, 197.
    See also Jesus Christ
Church, 158, 159, 198–99
Clemens, Samuel [pseud. Mark
    Twain], 8
Clinic, medical, 226–27
Cockroach, 79–80, 81
Coincidence, 3
Communication, 166, 200. *See*
    also Talk(ing); Write
    (writers, writing)
Community, 176, 196
Compassion, 160, 243
Competition, 68
Complaining, 47, 58, 164
Computer programming, 39
Confidence, 15, 24, 33
    self-, 14, 186
Consciousness
    clash between states of, 150

expanding, 201
heavenly states of, 20
higher state of, 7, 21, 149,
    208, 243
human. *See* Human: con-
    sciousness
Contact lenses, 203–4
Contemplation. *See also* Spiri-
    tual Exercises of ECK;
    Technique(s)
    experiences in, 138–39, 171, 204
    going into, 24–25, 166
    seeing Light during, 35
    on truth, 202
Control factor, 224
Co-worker(s)
    with God, 98, 107, 112, 168
    with the Mahanta, 112, 119
    serve as, 120. *See also* Service
Cows, 150–51
Creative (creativity), 39, 186, 189
    challenge, 101
    pursuits, 197
    of Soul, 6, 102, 104
Cricket. *See* Sound(s): of a
    cricket
Criticism, 13, 128, 186
Crossroads, 224–25
Crown chakra, 202–3
Curtain
    layers of, 130, 132–33
    pulling back, 129, 133, 207–8
Cycle, 97, 147

Dating, 56
Daydream(s), 180, 182–83, 197
Death, 44–45. *See also* Transla-
    tion
    before coming into ECK, 119
    fear of, 44, 229
    of loved one, 159–60
    near-, experience, 229
Debt(s), 12, 196
Decisions, 186
Depression, 24, 45–47, 50–51
Desire. *See* Longing

Detachment, 82, 151, 239–41
Determination, 8
Dethrone, 187
Deus ex machina, 188–89
Direct perception, 130
Discipline, 219
  self-, 128, 152
Discourses. *See* ECKANKAR:
  discourses
Disney, Walt, 100–104
Doctor, 153–55, 226–27. *See
  also* Chiropractor
Dog(s) 33–35, 136, 191, 240–41
Doubt(s), 115, 121, 186
Dream(s). *See also*
  Daydream(s); Golden-
  tongued Wisdom
  books on, 63
  categories of, 179–80, 197
  about the end of the world,
    222–23
  experience, 191, 198, 211,
    212, 224
  helping others in, 44–45
  initiation, 180, 183–84, 197
  of inner worlds, 49–50
  of intrusion, 180, 184–88, 197
  journal, 191–92
  life, 179
  life is a, 215
  with Light and Sound, 180,
    197, 211
  with the Mahanta, 180, 183,
    197, 198, 210–12
  meeting Master(s) in, 183,
    212, 228–29
  message in, 12, 29–31
  misunderstanding, 49, 185
  of past, 23, 224
  people acting out of character
    in, 184–85
  of realization, 208
  of release from fear, 180, 197
  researching, 179
  script, 187
  state, 21, 44, 179, 210, 212

  study, 192
  symbology, 179, 224
  travel, 130
  of understanding, 180, 197,
    207–9, 210
  vivid, 48
  waking, 180, 197, 201–5,
    219–21, 231
  world, 185, 186, 191
Dream Master, 21, 31, 63
Dreamer, 184, 185, 186, 206,
  207, 209
  in ECK, 191
  eternal, 179, 180, 195, 202
Dry spell, 192

Earth, 110, 112
ECK, 125. *See also* Teaching(s):
  ECK
  action of, 2
  afraid to talk about, 21
  awareness of, 130
  Blue Light of, 171–72
  community, 176
  Current, 123
  dependence upon, 147
  devotion to, 8
  flow of, 8
  help from, 57, 76
  hungry for, 109, 110
  Initiator, 184
  introduction to, 111
  love of, 243
  linkup with, 184, 243
  manifestations of, 1
  message of. *See* Message: the
    ECK
  path of, 4, 14, 23, 59, 96, 98,
    110, 164, 176, 179, 206
  purpose of, 19
  resistance to, 153
  Satsang class. *See* Satsang
    class
  sounds of. *See* Sound(s): of
    ECK
  talking about, 22

250

HU
  Chant, 85, 210, 211
  chanting, 35, 66, 67, 110–11,
    114, 138, 160–61, 212, 227,
    231
  sound of, 212
Human
  consciousness, 103, 117, 118,
    208
  nature, 101
Humility, 72, 79, 80, 147
Humor, 27
Hunch, 8
Hurricane, 114

Illness(es), 111, 151, 152,
    226–27, 229, 238
Illusion(s), 45, 157, 180
Images, 7, 147, 206, 211
Imagination, 138, 160
Individual, 1, 22, 143
Initiate report, 50, 51, 61
Initiation, 84, 143, 184. *See also*
    Dream(s): initiation
Initiator, ECK. *See* ECK:
    Initiator
Inner Master. *See also* Dream
    Master; Mahanta; Wah Z
  gives true message of ECK,
    242
  help from, 219, 230
  instructions from, 59, 228
  as matrix of Light and Sound,
    122, 138
  presence of, 217, 219
  protection of. *See* Protect(ion):
    of the Mahanta
Inquisition, Spanish, 21
Insight(s), 202, 207, 224. *See
    also* Golden-tongued
    Wisdom
Inspiration, 6
*In the Company of ECK
    Masters,* 174, 181
Intrusion, 185–88, 231. *See also*
    Dream(s): of intrusion

Intuition, 59, 100

Jealousy, 185
Jesus Christ, 90, 91, 174, 175,
    181
Jesus Christ, Superstar, 175
Journal, 192. *See also* Dream(s):
    journal
Journey
  home to God, 143, 145, 221
  inner, 140
  of Soul, 143, 149, 225
"Journey Home, The," 147, 148,
    241–42
Journey of Soul, Mahanta
    Transcripts, Book 1, 174
Joy, 149
Judging, 62, 127
Justice, 5

Kangaroos, 105–6
Karma (karmic)
  balance, 62
  comes back, 217
  creating, 60
  earning and paying own, 4,
    49, 96
  instant, 16
  Law of. *See* Law(s): of Karma
  overload, 151
  patterns, 197
  seeds, 117
  speeding up, 215
  transfer, 151
  understanding, 149
  unnecessary, 120
Keys, 107
Keystone of ECK, 242–43
Kindness, 160
Kittens, 32
Klemp, Sri Harold. *See*
    Mahanta; Wah Z

Language of Minnesota. *See*
    Minnesota
Laughter, 139, 140

Trouble(s), 146, 218, 227, 228
Trust, 13, 24
  in the ECK, 14, 27
  the Inner Master, 14–15
  Mahanta's guidance, 11
Truth
  accompanied by Light, 133
  curtain hides, 129
  is ever new, 65
  living, 35, 128
  put in perspective, 175
  Spirit of the unwritten, 116,
    122
  talking about, 70
Twain, Mark. *See* Clemens,
    Samuel
Twitchell, Paul, 86, 105, 143,
    144, 145
Typesetter, 116

Umbrellas, 235
Understand(ing)
  characteristics of God-
    Realized person, 6
  dreams of. *See* Dream(s): of
    understanding
  among ECK initiates, 78
  life, 40
  Light and Sound of God, 1, 172
  problems, 152
  spiritual realities, 130
Unfoldment, 59, 168, 227

Vanity, 13–14, 181
Vehicle for ECK. *See*
    Channel(s): for ECK
Veils, 208. *See also* Curtain
Vibration, 211
Video game(s), 56, 57, 60, 97
Video parlor(s), 55, 57, 96–97,
    233
Viewpoint, 183, 184
Visa, 43
Vision(s), 7, 102, 204
Visualize (visualization), 28,
    106, 227, 231

Voice(s)
  of the ECK, 145
  of God, 94, 132, 148, 239
  of the Inner Master, 15

Wah Z, 28, 138, 139, 159
Wall hangings, 204
Warning(s), 11–12
Washcloth, 32, 33
Watch, 15, 16
Watcher, becoming the, 6–7
Watch-repair story, 40–42
Water-on-the-ceiling story, 203
Weather forecaster, 50
Westminster Abbey, 65, 66
Whale story, 208–9
Williams, Hank, 121, 122
Wind
  of ECK, 113–14, 128
  from Heaven, 130
  from the mountain, 125, 128,
    137, 140
Window. *See* Experience:
    window to; Soul: window of
Wisdom, 40, 107, 243
Wolf (wolves), 7–8, 87, 88
Word, 8
  of God, 36, 133, 149
World(s). *See also* Plane(s)
  Astral, 206
  end of the, 222
  inner, 187
  lower, 168, 190
  other, 109
  spiritual, 125
Writer's Digest, 182
Write (writers, writing) 8, 117,
    182–83

Year
  of the Arahata, 42
  of the Shariyat, First, 40, 42,
    81, 91

Zeal, 93
Zikar, 106

How to Learn More about ECKANKAR
Religion of the Light and Sound of God

Why are you as important to God as any famous head of state, priest, minister, or saint that ever lived?

- Do you know God's purpose in your life?
- Why does God's Will seem so unpredictable?
- Why do you talk to God, but practice no one religion?

ECKANKAR can show you why special attention from God is neither random nor reserved for the few known saints. But it is for every individual. It is for anyone who opens himself to Divine Spirit, the Light and Sound of God.

People want to know the secrets of life and death. In response to this need Sri Harold Klemp, today's spiritual leader of ECKANKAR, and Paul Twitchell, its modern-day founder, have written a series of monthly discourses that give the Spiritual Exercises of ECK. They can lead Soul in a direct way to God.

Those who wish to study ECKANKAR can receive these special monthly discourses which give clear, simple instructions for the spiritual exercises.

Membership in ECKANKAR Includes

1. Twelve monthly discourses which include information on Soul, the spiritual meaning of dreams, Soul Travel techniques, and ways to establish a personal relationship with Divine Spirit. You may study them alone at home or in a class with others.
2. The *Mystic World,* a quarterly newsletter with a Wisdom Note and articles by the Living ECK Master. In it are also letters and articles from students of ECKANKAR around the world.
3. Special mailings to keep you informed of upcoming ECKANKAR seminars and activities worldwide, new study materials available from ECKANKAR, and more.
4. The opportunity to attend ECK Satsang classes and book discussions with others in your community.
5. Initiation eligibility.
6. Attendance at certain meetings for members of ECKANKAR at ECK seminars.

How to Find Out More

To request membership in ECKANKAR using your credit card (or for a free booklet on membership) call (612) 544-0066, weekdays, between 8:00 a.m. and 5:00 p.m., central time. Or write to: ECKANKAR, Att: Information, P.O. Box 27300, Minneapolis, MN 55427 U.S.A.

Introductory Books on ECKANKAR

Unlocking the Puzzle Box
Mahanta Transcripts, Book 6
Harold Klemp

Life is like a puzzle box with parts of it locked away from your understanding. Now you can open the box and begin to solve the mystery of life for yourself. When you open your heart and mind, the Light and Sound of God can lift you in consciousness to a greater life. This book shows you how.

Earth to God, Come In Please . . .

This anthology is filled with stories from ordinary people who have become aware of a greater force operating in their lives. Their experiences outside the commonplace brought lessons in love and spiritual freedom that changed them deeply. They show how we can make contact with the Voice of God, for spiritual knowledge and awareness beyond words.

The Secret Language of Waking Dreams
Mike Avery

Are you overlooking the countless ways life speaks to you for your benefit? This book guides you to a better understanding of your own secret inner language—the language of waking dreams. It will wake you up to what life is really trying to teach you!

HU: A Love Song to God
Audiocassette

A wonderful introduction to ECKANKAR, this two-tape set is designed to help listeners of any religious or philosophical background benefit from the gifts of the HU. It includes an explanation of the HU, stories about how the HU works in daily life, and exercises to uplift you spiritually.

For fastest service, phone (612) 544-0066 weekdays between 8:00 a.m. and 5:00 p.m., central time, to request books using your credit card, or look under **ECKANKAR** in your phone book for an ECKANKAR Center near you. Or write: **ECKANKAR, Att: Information, P.O. Box 27300, Minneapolis, MN 55427 U.S.A.**

There May Be an
ECKANKAR Study Group near You

ECKANKAR offers a variety of local and international activities for the spiritual seeker. With hundreds of study groups worldwide, ECKANKAR is near you! Many areas have ECKANKAR Centers where you can browse through the books in a quiet, unpressured environment, talk with others who share an interest in this ancient teaching, and attend beginning discussion classes on how to gain the attributes of Soul: wisdom, power, love, and freedom.

Around the world, ECKANKAR study groups offer special one-day or weekend seminars on the basic teachings of ECKANKAR. Check your phone book under **ECKANKAR**, or call **(612) 544-0066** for membership information and the location of the ECKANKAR Center or study group nearest you. Or write **ECKANKAR, Att: Information, P.O. Box 27300, Minneapolis, MN 55427 U.S.A.**

☐ Please send me information on the nearest ECKANKAR discussion or study group in my area.

☐ Please send me more information about membership in ECKANKAR, which includes a twelve-month spiritual study.

Reno ECKANKAR Center
351 E. Taylor
Reno, NV 89502
323-3623

Please type or print clearly

941

Name _____

Street _____ Apt. # _____

City _____ State/Prov. _____

Zip/Postal Code _____ Country _____